S0-BRQ-893

WITHDRAWN
L. R. COLLEGE LIBRARY

THE WOUNDED DON'T CRY

THE WOUNDED DON'T CRY

by

QUENTIN REYNOLDS

1941

E. P. DUTTON & CO., INC.

NEW YORK

Lenoir Rhyne College
LIBRARY

940.5
R33w

COPYRIGHT 1940
BY CROWELL-COLLIER PUBLISHING CO.
COPYRIGHT 1941
BY QUENTIN REYNOLDS

First printing............January, 1941
Second printing..........January, 1941
Third printing...........January, 1941
Fourth printing..........January, 1941
Fifth printing...........January, 1941
Sixth printing...........January, 1941
Seventh printing.........January, 1941
Eighth printing..........January, 1941
Ninth printing...........January, 1941
Tenth printing...........January, 1941
Eleventh printing........February, 1941
Twelfth printing.........February, 1941
Thirteenth printing......February, 1941
Fourteenth printing......February, 1941
Fifteenth printing.......February, 1941
Sixteenth printing.......February, 1941
Seventeenth printing.....February, 1941

17860
April, 1941.

PRINTED IN THE UNITED STATES OF AMERICA
AMERICAN BOOK–STRATFORD PRESS, INC., NEW YORK

To My Neighbors:

THE PEOPLE OF LONDON

FOREWORD

I DECIDED to write this book four months ago, while lying under a freight car. The freight car was on a siding which led to a dock at Pointe de Graves. I was waiting to get a ship for England. Pointe de Graves isn't much of a place. It is about sixty miles from Bordeaux at the mouth of the Gironde River. It has a dock, a monument commemorating the arrival of American troops in 1917 and a railroad spur. Anchored out somewhere in the harbor there were an English cruiser and two Dutch freighters. When dawn came a small boat was to take me to one of the Dutch freighters which would then go to England.

It was a brilliant night and the moon gleamed whitely on the neat, roofless dock. The dock had been built after the war as part of the Reparations Plan. It had been built by a German engineer, and when he had finished building it he had said bitterly, "Well, I have built your dock for you because I was forced to build it. But I promise you that one day I will come back and destroy it."

An English sentry, standing on the dock, had told me that. We had both laughed a little but not too heartily. It was a fact that bombers had come over the night before and had dropped bombs within a quarter of a mile of the dock. But they may have been aiming for the English cruiser. We had laughed and then I'd crawled into a sleeping bag, used my typewriter for a pillow, and tried to sleep. The mosquitoes were very bad. A sleeping bag doesn't cover your face. The mosquitoes buzzed and buzzed and then there was a louder, even more persistent buzzing which wasn't a mosquito. The German motors sing a throaty contralto. The French and English planes sing a high tune. They are strictly Johnny-one-note crooners. They sound much like the buzzing of a bee. These were German bombers all right.

Vague forms around me were getting out of sleeping bags leisurely. There were thirteen of us scattered on the dock and near the dock. We pulled on our shoes and stretched and yawned and slapped mosquitoes, and then looked around. The bombers were getting closer now and from their sound we could tell they were very low. I moved back from the dock fifty yards. It was then that I saw the freight car. Usually you lie in a ditch when bombers are near. But there were no ditches here.

The planes were almost directly overhead now and the guns started to spit bullets up into the night. There is always danger of being hit by one of these when it comes down. One fell two feet from me and I heard it land with a clink on a stone. So I crawled under the freight train. A freight train is a fine shelter. It protects you from falling shrapnel, and it protects you from bomb fragments. I lay there between the wheels and it wasn't very comfortable. Sharp grass sprang up from between the railroad ties and the mosquitoes were annoying. I'd change my position and find hard gravel and that wasn't good either.

I had slept in a bed only once during the past eight days. Sleeping in fields and on hard floors isn't bad at first, but gradually you develop a thousand sore spots. Your side and your hips protest very vigorously after a few nights. Except for that one night, I hadn't had my clothes off either, and that never makes you feel better. I had been coming from Paris, always staying one jump ahead of the Germans, and it had been a hard trip. I lay there under the freight car feeling sorry for myself. A bomb fell perhaps half a mile away and then another fell closer. The planes were flying up and down this part of the coast, giving it a good going over; looking, I imagine, for the English cruiser.

I was feeling sorry for myself. What the hell was I doing here under this freight car?

Then the night was lit up with a brilliance that turned it into daylight. A bomber had dropped a flare. Its light completely banished the night for a moment and then the bomb came. This was one of the half-ton bombs. It landed perhaps three hundred yards away. It is impossible to describe the incredible loudness of a bomb. It is all the claps of thunder you have ever heard rolled into one roaring crescendo. After its first sharp explosion there is a sort of rumbling for a moment, as though the bomb were growling because it had missed you. Then an over-powering silence. Perhaps that's because you are deafened a little. Then you hear the humming of the planes again. You must remember that this was June 29, 1940. This was before the real Battle of London began. Fools like myself thought that this was the worst that could happen. I was grateful for this bomb. Now I knew what I was doing there under the freight car. I laughed at myself for having been such a fool. I had a front row seat at the biggest show ever staged. What was I doing under the freight car? I wouldn't be anywhere else in the world. If I were in New York I would have been miserable knowing that others were covering this war and I wasn't. If I were in Hollywood I'd be talking of the war and envying those who were there, actually seeing it. I wasn't sorry for myself now. I was sorry for my colleagues at *Collier's,* who weren't with me.

It had gotten better. The anti-aircraft guns were firing rapidly now. They sounded very small and very futile. Now and then another bomb would fall and for the moment overshadow the barking of the guns. The humming of the planes was the melody in this symphony. It was always there when the bombs and the guns died down. And then suddenly, the bombing stopped. The guns barked a few times in angry disappointment, the hum of the planes grew fainter and fainter, and once again Pointe de Graves was nothing but a dock, a railroad siding and a monument commemorating the arrival of American troops in 1917.

Once again the moonlight bathed the dock and the monument whitely, and now you could hear the soft lapping of small waves against the dock and the shore. It was then that I decided to write this book. Years from now, when I'm tired perhaps of being a reporter, I'll read it and remember the terrific exaltation I felt this night under the freight car. If I become jaded and begin to take my job for granted and think that it is a futile, useless job, I'll read this and know better. I'll remember that I had a ring-side seat to watch the greatest fight ever staged.

I must put it all down quickly before I forget it. Barry Faris, the International News Service chief, used to tell me, "Stories are like vegetables. Use them quickly or they spoil." He was right.

And so this book.

London,
November 1, 1940.

CONTENTS

Contents

THE WOUNDED DON'T CRY

CHAPTER ONE

I'LL CABLE THE PRESIDENT . . .

I ARRIVED IN PARIS on May 10, 1940, which wasn't
bad timing. Hitler marched into Belgium just as I
marched into the Ritz Bar. The first thing I did was
to order a drink. I don't know what Hitler did first.

A month before, the theater of war had moved to
Norway. In New York we mistakenly believed that
perhaps the war would be fought in Norway. Looking back it seems pretty stupid but we weren't alone.
Those magnificent armchair domestic foreign correspondents who tell us via radio just what is going to
happen were all excited about Norway. Even the
sober authentic correspondents in London believed
that the English Government would make every effort to defend Norway. "Every effort" meant that
the whole navy would swing into action; that the still
untested air force would go to work and the army
would put down its tea and take up a bayonet. But
we all lived in a fool's paradise in those blissful days
when it was still a "phoney" war.

Charlie Colebaugh, the Managing Editor of *Col-*

lier's, woke me one morning very early. I've always believed that telephone calls which are made before noon aren't worth listening to. This was an exception. It wasn't very long.

"Get to Norway," Charlie said.

"Norway? How the hell do you go to Norway?" I was still half asleep.

"That's your little problem," he said and hung up.

"Pack my things, I'm going to Norway," I yelled at my plump, motherly maid.

"Right away," she said soothingly and brought me a glass of Alka-Seltzer.

The problem of getting to Norway wasn't as easy as the travel advertisements might lead one to believe. You couldn't go directly. I cabled London and found that the Government was not allowing any correspondents to follow the army to the scene of the fighting. A long while afterwards we found out why. There were some correspondents there already. Leland Stowe was earning the Pulitzer Prize by his magnificent stories from Oslo. Whether he'll actually get it or not doesn't matter. We, his colleagues, have already awarded it to him and knowing Lee I dare say he'd rather have the admiration of his colleagues (which he has—one hundred per cent) than have a scroll with his name emblazoned on it.

We finally decided that I'd go by way of Germany. The German army was being very tender with neutral correspondents then. Then too, I'd worked in Berlin and knew enough German to tell a wiener schnitzel from a Reichsoberregierungsrat.

It was a matter of hours to get my passport okayed by the Secretary of State and then I blithely walked into the office of the German Consulate General. There might be a delay of a day or two, he told me suavely, but in these days as a matter of form they had to make application to Berlin. It didn't turn out to be a matter of form. Two days later I was told that my visa had been denied. From a pipe-line I had into the Consulate I found out that the Gestapo had sent back just one word about me, "undesirable." Pressed for details by the Consulate General, who seemed honestly anxious to facilitate things, it developed that two stories I had written the year before had come to the attention of the Gestapo. They were "Portrait of a Murderer," the story of young Herschel Grynszpan who had killed Ernst von Rath, the third secretary of the German Embassy in Paris; the other was a story on the Jewish persecutions called "Unwanted." So I never got to Germany. But I will. It may take a long time before I march in behind the English Army, but some day we'll march under the Brandenburg Tor on Unter den Linden and a lot of us have made a pledge as to just what we are going to do when we pass under that war memorial.

I aimed for London. I went on the *Conte di Savoia* to Naples and then overland to Paris. There were only seventy passengers on the lovely ship, which meant that we each had a steward to wait on us. This seemed to be a very comfortable war back in those dim days of April, 1940. There was a man named Graves Smith on board and because he was the only other person around who liked to sit up after dark we became quite friendly. He was in the rubber business and was on his way to England to buy some.

"How much rubber you going to buy?" I asked him.

"All they got," Smith said calmly.

He taught me a lot about the rubber business. It seems that you sell rubber before you buy it. You sell it for delivery next year and then you hustle around the world looking for it, trying to buy it at a cheaper price than the price for which you've sold it. It seemed a silly way to do business to me.

"I've got a stock market system something like that," I told him. "It never misses."

He perked up his ears. "What is it?"

"I buy on Monday, sell on Friday," I told him airily.

He looked thoughtful. "I don't get it," he said.

"It's easy to explain," I told him. "Actually, Smith, writing is just a hobby to me. I'm really a Wall Street operator on a big scale. By buying on Monday it is obvious that any inflation is immediately prevented and then owing to government demands for money, conversion to stabilize would increase the floating debt way out of proportion. But if you sell on Friday what happens? Now the diversion of expenditure is gradual and the manipulation of convertible bonds can be liquidated, that is, of course, provided there are no interlocking directorates. If there are inter-locking directorates then of course it is entirely different. Then I usually buy on Wednesday morning and sell in April."

"Will you have another drink?" Smith said.

Smith told me about a subsidiary company in which he was interested. I thought he was giving me the same kind of double talk I'd been giving him until he showed me a prospectus and letters dealing with it. He and several associates had formed a company for the purpose of manufacturing artificial rubber breasts. There were, Smith explained, several such articles on the market; in fact he named half a dozen film stars (female) who were regular customers. But there was one thing lacking; those now on the market had to be strapped in the back or they wouldn't stay in place. The gay deceivers which his company was already manufacturing would be cup-shaped on the inside and would stay in place by suction. A woman could wear a backless evening gown and no one would be the wiser.

"Best of all," Smith said earnestly, "we can make them for a few cents and sell them quite cheaply. And they are all chocolate flavored."

I rolled my head with that punch. "I should think if you could get the natural . . ."

"Listen. I'm not kidding," Smith said. "Rubber in its crude state has a very definite odor. Chocolate is the strongest deodorant known to the trade. By mixing peppermint or clove . . ."

"There's a rock outside, let's go out and look at it," I told Smith.

"What's a rock doing out in the ocean?" he said warily.

"It's a rock called Gibraltar put up by the Prudential Insurance Company." We went out and looked at the rock.

It went like that all the way to Paris. We had a lot of fun. The weather was nice; life was good. By now the wireless told us that the balloon had gone up and come down in Norway. It looked as though I were in for a soft assignment. Naturally the Germans wouldn't dare to attack Belgium and Holland. And of course the Maginot Line was impregnable. Heigh-ho! Paris would be fun and I'd run over to London for a couple of weeks and play around with Arthur Christiansen, the editor of the *Express,* and Frank Owen who ran the *Standard* and Sidney Bernstein and Nat Gubbins, to me the world's funniest writer, and Ewart Hodgson and Paul Holt and the rest of Fleet Street. I was at home in Fleet Street. Yes, this was the life. And on an expense account too. It seemed too good to be true. . . .

So I walked into the Ritz Bar on May 10th and I've been running in circles ever since. First I ran toward the front; then away from it and since then I've been running away from bombs and that's mighty wearing on the feet.

Before you can cover a war you have to be accredited to the fighting forces. Getting accredited to the French Army during the Spring of 1940 was a little bit like getting into the Kingdom of Heaven on a bicycle. The long thin line of red tape which finally strangled France began at the top, coiled in thoroughly illogical circles all over the place and then wound up in that gloomy building which had once been the Hotel Continental. Until the Bureau Central Militaire de la Circulation and its ill-begotten child the Ministry of Information began to operate in that gloomy building, Red Tape was only in its infancy. Never before had such a compendium of dreary and confused minds ever been assembled under one roof. They had plenty of paper, lots of pencils, hundreds of rubber stamps and minds as blank as the white cliffs of Calais. They were meticulously polite and they were glad to see you whenever you dropped in but they were a bit slow on getting things done.

There is an old political adage which says "If you can't lick 'em, jine 'em." I always operate on that basis. Ken Downs, an old friend of mine, was in charge of the International News Service in Paris. Because Downs filed dispatches about every hour while my stories went out at most once a week I couldn't beat Downs. So I joined him. Within two hours of the time I arrived in Paris, Downs took me to the Hotel Continental to apply for my accreditization. Monsieur Pierre Comert, Press Liaison officer for the Foreign Office who took care of these things was charming.

"First you must get a letter from the American Ambassador," he explained. "Then get six photographs of yourself. Fill out this form and then come back. I am sure it can be arranged."

Within two hours I had the six pictures; I had a letter from Ambassador Bullitt; I had filled out the necessary forms (in triplicate) and I had been fitted for a uniform. The French insisted upon all correspondents wearing uniforms when visiting the front. Their reasoning was sound. The front even then was always under observation by the Germans. If they saw a man in civilian clothes mingling with the French soldiers they might think him to be a Cabinet Minister and send some bombing planes over to get him.

I returned to Monsieur Comert. He was all smiles and full of courtesy. "Phone me in a few days," he said. "I'll try to hurry it through."

I phoned him the following day. He was a little unhappy at my hurry.

"These things take time," he said mournfully. "First your application goes to the Deuxième Bureau, then it must go to the War Office. It may take three weeks or a month."

"So it's like that?" I said.

"Yes, it is like that," Monsieur Comert said softly.

I went into a huddle with myself. There wasn't a story in Paris worth writing. I wanted to get to the front and I couldn't get out of Paris until I was accredited. I came out of the huddle with an idea. I wrote out a cable and stuck it in my pocket. Then I went to see Monsieur Comert again. He looked a little pained when I walked into his office.

"I just want some advice, Monsieur Comert," I said very humbly. "I am sending a cable to President

Roosevelt asking him to cable Premier Reynaud to facilitate my accreditization. I don't want to go over your head, however. And I suppose the censor will have to read my cable. It is rather a personal one and I wonder if you wouldn't take it on yourself to censor it."

I handed him the cable I had typed out. He read it with startled eyes, as well he might. The cable read: "Dear Uncle Franklin, am having difficulty getting accredited to French Army. Time is important. Would you phone or cable Premier Reynaud and ask him to hurry things up. It was grand of you to phone me last night. Please give my love to Aunt Eleanor. Quent."

Monsieur Comert was speechless for a moment. "You are a nephew of the President?" he said in awe. "But of course, Quentin Reynolds—Quentin Roosevelt. I suppose Quentin is an old family name. Well, now imagine you being the President's nephew. . . ."

"I never talk about it," I said modestly. "I prefer to get along on my own. Really, I wish you wouldn't mention it to anyone."

"Of course not," he said hastily. "This changes everything. I'll get right on the phone and fix things up."

"Good. Then I won't bother sending the cable." I put out my hand to take it off his desk.

"Ah no," he said smiling. "Let me send it for you. I will send it through government channels. It will reach the White House much quicker that way."

I winced at that. I could imagine Margaret Le

Hand or Steve Early opening it, reading it, and wondering who this madman was who called the President "Uncle Franklin." But I couldn't withdraw now. In any case within twenty-four hours I got my precious pink card which read: *"Quentin Reynolds, Nationalité Américaine. Est autorisé à circuler dans la zone des armées français en fonction des exigences de sa mission de reporter aux armées. Correspondent de guerre accredité par le G.Q.G."*

I was accredited to the French Army. Now I could go to work.

CHAPTER TWO

THE CHAMPAGNE WAS WARM . . .

THERE WERE PROBABLY a hundred English and
American correspondents accredited to the French
Army. They divided us into three groups and took us
on organized sorties. If we had cars of our own we
drove them. Ken Downs had a magnificent new Ford.
He and Bob Cooper of the London *Times* and I
teamed up. We made a good combination because no
one of us was opposition to the other. Our group was
told that it had been arranged for us to visit the
front-line airdromes. It seemed like a grand trip and
the prospect of getting a good story seemed bright.

Our first stop was an airdrome not far from Chantilly. The actual fighting, of course, was going on
fifty miles north, but this was considered to be one
of the front-line airdromes. It was well camouflaged.
It had once been a track for the training of horses.
Now dull gray airplanes hid under the leafy trees
which bordered the track. The General in charge
was all right. He explained how his particular com-

27

mand operated. Then—it was a warm morning—he asked us into the squadron mess.

The General apologized because the champagne wasn't iced. Champagne is not the ordinary ration of fighting pilots at airdromes near the front. Nor do you usually associate champagne with dugouts and sandbags piled high and a dozen uniformed, tired men leaning wearily against a makeshift bar. But visitors are rare in the region of the front and fighting men like to have a convivial drink.

The General was short and stocky and he had none of the stuffed dignity of the peacetime general. His Croix de Guerre had sixteen palms on it; he had downed twenty-eight planes in the last war. He sipped his wine and talked proudly, affectionately about the men who stood with us in the large, well-lighted dugout.

"You don't hear so much of our French fighting planes," he said. "It's because our pilots are team-workers. Our fighters have two jobs: protection and destruction. They protect other airforce units and land units. They destroy bombers and reconnaissance enemy planes. They are wonderful, really, and as for the British pilots, oh! they are great!" He was a tough, blunt general who talked the language of his men; who drank wine with his men; whose eyes met theirs with sympathy and affection.

There was a tall, dark lad named Paul. An hour earlier he had downed his third Dornier. The rest of them were kidding him about what they called

his blind flying. When I asked him what they meant
he explained ruefully,

"This morning I was up there flying through a
cloud," he said, "when without any warning, a big
bomber loomed in front of me. Neither of us had
time to shoot. I just zoomed over him, almost scrap-
ing his wings. Then I turned and went after him.
But the sky was full of clouds and I couldn't see him.
Just on a hunch I kept firing in one direction and
then I heard an explosion. I'd gotten him all right,
though I never did see him. He crashed only five
kilometers from here."

These fighting men worked long hours. They
started at 4 A.M. and worked until eight at night. The
rest of the time they were of course, subject to call.

They all looked tired, but grim. They were up
against it and they knew it, but they knew too that
they were fighting not only for their own lives but
for the life of their country. Because they were usually outnumbered four or five to one they had of
necessity become great pilots and terrific shots. "That
Joseph now," the General laughed. "He has the
Croix Noir in his eyes."

Joseph, the Alsatian, sheepishly grinned at what
his general had said. The others looked at him with
a little awe. He did seem to have the black cross of
the German air force in his eyes. Every time he went
up he found some enemy aircraft. He had come back
that morning with a sorry-looking ship. His Morane
had been riddled with bullets. They counted 331
bullet holes and two cannon holes in it. But some-

how or other he had landed safely, had taken another ship and had gone up to get two more Germans.

"It sounded," Joseph said unexpectedly, "as though I were a kettledrum and they were playing me. It went 'boom, boom, boom.' Then my ship started to fall apart so I came home. Look, your glass is empty."

A dozen pilots looked unhappy and disturbed. The glass of a visitor should never be anything but full. But we left.

Outside the dugout there was a space, perhaps four feet square, and a pilot with six palms on his Croix de Guerre was bending over it anxiously. He had just tacked a sign on a pole. It read: "Watch out for the flowers."

"How can they come up if people step on them?" he asked seriously. "They wouldn't be up for another month anyway," he added.

Another month? There were a hundred men and a hundred planes in this particular group. How many would be there in another month?

We went to Chantilly, two miles away. There was an inn there with a garden and we sat there drinking coffee. Only the ancient proprietor and his wife were left. Everyone else had been evacuated. The sun bathed the garden and a cool breeze brought the scent of honeysuckle from the nearby forest. It was no day for death to show her ugly head. But she did.

First I heard the bombs. They were like off-stage noises heard faintly. But they got closer and louder and now fifteen specks, silver against the blue of the sky, appeared. They were up about ten thousand feet. Tiny, black, harmless-looking dots dropped from them: half-ton messages from eternity.

It was the first time I had ever heard bombs explode. I thought and was thrilled by the fact that they had landed very close. Actually the nearest had landed on the airdrome we had just left; a mile away. I didn't realize then that my apartment in London would catch three direct hits within two weeks only a few short months later. This seemed very thrilling at the time and safe enough, too. Now it has ceased being thrilling and it has ceased being safe. It's only horrible now—then it was thrilling.

To get back to Chantilly. The bombers veered north. The anti-aircraft began but the sharp flashes found only blue sky. Now the roar of the fighting planes inserted a new note in this symphony of thunder. They roared up, trying to gain altitude quickly. They circled, their noses pointing high, as high as they could point without going into a spin. Six of them wheeled into formation and lit out after the bombers, hardly distinguishable now. Six against fifteen! The fighters were streaking across the sky after their prey. Then they too disappeared. The garden was quiet again but the breeze didn't bring the scent of honeysuckle. It brought a sharp, pungent small. Here and there on the horizon lazy spirals of black smoke appeared. I debated whether to go back. It would be better to think that those fighting men, whose only worry was my empty glass and flowers that shouldn't be stepped on, were all safe.

We met eight French air generals that day. All were magnificent. It is the custom now to decry everything that the French Army or air force did. But I don't know one correspondent who spent any time at the French front who has anything but admiration for the way the fighting men of France conducted themselves. The French Army didn't collapse from below—the French air force never collapsed. The outmoded planes they were forced to use collapsed and there came a time when there was no ammunition for their guns—but the pilots themselves put it out until the last. I was there.

I met a handsome Corsican who commanded one of the largest airdromes in the north. He was hobbling painfully on a stick and I asked him the obvious question.

"No, not wounded," he said ruefully. "Just a touch of gout."

A few moments later I stood beside him and watched his group take off. Bombers had been heard operating not far off. The pilots, looking grotesque in their heavily padded suits and their heavy helmets and fantastic goggles, climbed into the two-seater Potezes, the one-man Moranes and Blochs; mechanics whirled propellers and they were off. They took off three at a time and within five minutes thirty of them were in the air. Some flew to the northeast where bombers had been reported. Three of them flew directly north. I questioned the commander with my eyes. "Reconnaissance," he said briefly. "We want information."

An hour later two of those three planes came back. One youngster rushed from his plane as soon as it landed. He looked very tired but triumphant. He had a package of notes in his hand. "How is it going?"

He shrugged his shoulders. "It's tough going."

It was tough going. At the time we never realized how tough it was. We were greatly impressed with the air force of France that lovely afternoon late in May. The pilots looked as though they had just stepped out of Hell's Angels or Wings. They were all good-looking and nonchalant and they flew their little airplanes beautifully. We were just learning then about Messerschmitts. Everything being equal, even a Morane had the same chance against a Messerschmitt as a cow would have against a bull. It took us another month to learn that.

There had been about twenty of us in this particular trip. We returned to Paris and wrote our stories. The story of the afternoon made a nice feature. I blithely wrote three thousand words quoting the various air force generals; quoting and naming the ace pilots we had met and to whom we had talked. The next day I was informed that eight hundred words had been cut out of my story. I couldn't use any names. I couldn't describe the various airdromes. I couldn't describe the workings of a Potez or a Bloch. I pleaded. I yelled. I screamed. But the red tape of the censor was thick enough to drown even my voice. The others had the same experience.

Downs, Cooper and I were disgusted with or-

ganized sorties after that. And with the censor too.
We sat in the Ritz Bar feeling sorry for ourselves
and drinking champagne orange. Three days a week
no whiskey or brandy was sold in France. H. R.
Knickerbocker had just arrived in Paris from New
York. Knick was a great favorite with the French
Government because for years he had been throwing
verbal punches at Hitler and had written several
powerful articles pleading for America's immediate
entrance into the war. Knick was treated with very
soft gloves by even the moribund Ministry of Information. Knick was a friend of Reynaud's and of
Mandel. He could get just about what he wanted.

Bob Cooper told us that Knick and Tom Delmar
of the London *Express* had gotten permission to go
to the front alone. That made Bob and me mad.
Downs didn't mind much because Knick worked for
INS. But with the instinct of wanting to be the first
one at a fire, which burns in the heart of any good
reporter, Ken was a bit downcast.

"If only the three of us could get permission to
visit the front," Cooper said, "we could get some
grand stories."

Bob Cooper is the mildest man I ever met. He has
large blue eyes and a baby face. Let me hasten to
add that he is married and has two children. I
couldn't imagine Cooper really getting angry. He
was too damned nice. But I had an idea and if I
could get Bob good and mad . . .

"Another round of drinks," I said, and then ignoring Cooper, I turned to Downs. "I always thought

The Times was the greatest newspaper in England, Ken. I thought it was virtually the voice of the Government."

Ken caught my wink. "It used to be," he said sadly. "I can remember the time when a correspondent from *The Times* was practically God."

"I remember working in Berlin," I said, still ignoring Bob. "Norman Ebbutt and Douglas Reed of *The Times* got every facility they asked for, but they were two pretty tough guys. They stood up for their rights."

"I stand up for my rights, too," Cooper said sullenly.

"Nothing personal, Bob old boy," I said hastily. "Of course you stand up for your rights. It doesn't matter to me that Tom Delmar is up at the front now and you aren't. Sure let the *Express* get a beat. Who cares?"

"Funny though," Downs said, "to see the *Express* getting precedence over *The Times*."

"Oh, well, it can't be helped," I sighed.

We sat there waiting for the poison to sink in. Finally Cooper banged his glass on the table.

"They can't do that to me," he yelled. "I'm going to see Comert or Colonel Schieffere. By God, I'll see Reynaud if I have to."

"Give me the bill," I called. "All right, Bob, since you feel that way, Ken and I will go along with you. Ken has the car here."

He was still grumbling incoherently as we climbed into the car. Downs drove to the Hotel Continental in two minutes. If we could keep Bob mad he might pull it off. I kept prompting him.

"Churchill always gives his speeches to *The Times* in advance . . . *The Times* is more than a newspaper. *The Times* is England. It's a cricket field, it's a bowler hat, it's the spirit of . . . of . . ."

"Nelson, the spirit of Nelson," Downs broke in. "They can't insult *The Times* like that, Bob."

". . . And then tell him—" we were outside Comert's office now—"that we three always travel together. Say Ken and I own the car between us. We always travel together so he'll have to give you three passes."

The door opened and Downs began to whistle "God Save The King." We sat down and waited. We heard a loud, angry voice bellowing behind the closed door. We heard the soothing plaintive voice of M. Comert. Then there was silence. Finally the door opened and Cooper emerged. He had three pink slips in his hand.

We were off. We planned to meet at Downs' office in the rue Caumartin in an hour. We packed our knapsacks. A knapsack will hold a couple of shirts, a toilet kit, a half-dozen cans of sardines and chicken, and four bottles of brandy. Each of us, thinking that the others might neglect that all-important item had brought four bottles. Downs brought four bottles of wine. Cooper had four bottles of Johnny Walker, Black Label. We were off for Nancy and Verdun and the Ligne Maginot. We were off to the front.

It was a beautiful warm day and there's nothing

much wrong with the north of France either. We
hauled the top of the car down and took off our hats
and let the sun give us a going over. Life was good.
This was a good war. Of course we didn't know then
about the nightmare to come.

"Remember that rooster they had for a mascot at
that fighter squadron we visited?" Cooper said
drowsily.

"Do you want a rooster, Bob?" Downs and I
would have given him anything. "We just want you
to be happy, Bob."

"No, I don't want a rooster," he drawled. "But all
these squadrons have mascots. We ought to have a
mascot too."

We discussed what kind of mascot would be good
to have with us. We went through the animal and
vegetable kingdoms without agreeing on anything.
Then Cooper settled it with one brilliant stroke.

"A willing peasant," he said triumphantly. "That's
what we ought to have. Very blond and maybe about
twenty."

Downs and I could only gaze in awe at the genius
of Cooper. If he wished to have a willing peasant he
should have one. Then we heard an angry buzzing
not too far away. Ken put on the brakes and the car
screeched to a stop. We tumbled out hurriedly. The
Germans were machine-gunning a lot of cars lately.
There was a ditch alongside the road. We huddled
there. A dozen Heinkels were floating lazily overhead. But they didn't drop anything and soon they
went on.

We had four glorious days, but we never found a willing peasant for a mascot. We visited the front and we talked to German prisoners and we thought the French Army was wonderful. And once near Montmédy I spent an afternoon in a pillbox between the lines. . . .

CHAPTER THREE

FRONT SEAT IN FLANDERS . . .

PIERRE LAUGHED AND SAID, "The fools, they missed again. That is two hundred and five shells today."

We were in an advanced observation post on a hill and some distance away was another hill. A German battery was on that hill. It kept firing at the farmhouse in the valley. The farmhouse had a red roof and its sides were pure white. Only the chimney had suffered, but the farmhouse wore its crooked chimney in a very jaunty manner, as an amiable drunk wears a battered hat. This was a gallant farmhouse, perhaps because it knew that it had a whole German division worried.

Our little concrete-and-steel observation post was fooling everyone but the sun. It had been dug into the side of the hill and evergreens had been placed over the steel and the concrete. Sturdy scrub oak and fir trees had been planted in front of it. For the moment this post was the eyes of the army; at least of that part of the army that was defending this sector. Behind us were heavy French tanks and light

quick tanks, machine-gun detachments, heavy 155's
and lighter 75's.

We knew what was behind us all right. We knew
too that the Germans were in front of us. We could
see the flashes from their guns and sometimes through
our glasses we could see something move for a moment, but against the dark green foliage of the woods
we couldn't tell whether we had seen a tank or an
ammunition wagon.

Technically we were in what army people still
call No Man's Land. But we were very snug and
comfortable in our little pillbox and very safe too.
Pierre sat on one side of me and André on the other.
Bright young artillery sergeants, these two. There
were two slits through the steel and the concrete.
Each one was a foot long and ten inches wide.
Pierre and André talked and laughed but their eyes
never strayed from those slits. Hardly ever. I mentioned that our little nest was fooling everyone but
the sun.

André said, "In English you say it like this, you
say it is hot like hell?"

"You said it, kid, it is hot like hell." I wiped the
sweat from my forehead. André laughed and then
Pierre laughed as though they shared some secret
joke. They did share a joke. A swell joke. Pierre got
up and went back through the dark tunnel that led
to another part of our observation post.

Pierre came back. He had a large aluminum canteen with him and its sides were gleaming with cold
sweat. He had three tin cups with him. He laughed

and poured cold wine into the cups. I had met Pierre and André an hour before but we were pals now. They had accepted me.

"To what shall we drink?" Pierre said.

"To the little farmhouse," I said, and we all laughed and drank to the little farmhouse. We looked and it was still almost intact. The wine was cold and it was beautiful.

We sat in companionable silence watching the scene below us. The German guns were firing fast. We knew that a division of Germans had orders to break through. A division is 15,000 men. That's a lot of men. They were all there in front of us. Some were to the right, thousands of them were behind the hill from which the battery was firing. Thousands were to the left. The French guns were firing fast but we couldn't hear them as well; we were so much closer to the German guns. When a shell leaves a gun it whistles for perhaps five seconds. We could see the flashes of the German guns, hear the whistle and then hear the dull boom.

Cooper and Downs and I had split up. They had given each of us an accompanying officer to take care of us. The last five miles of my trip had to be made on foot. That wasn't good because it had rained the night before and the paths were ankle-deep in mud. The last two miles weren't easy. But they were interesting. A young lieutenant was with me. We'd cross a road and bump into a queer-looking concrete object; a pillbox commanding every horizon. Guns would bristle from a dozen slits in the concrete. An anti-tank ditch would stop us then. It meant destruction for any German tank that blundered into it.

Of course we didn't know then that General Corap's army was beginning to crack at Sedan and at Abbeville. We thought we were watching a great army. We didn't know that there weren't shells for those nice-looking guns. We didn't know that the General Staff had nothing at all to combat the sixty-ton tanks that would be coming over soon. We only knew that the soldiers were fine and that the officers we met were gay and friendly and that they were filled with confidence and with a fierce hatred of Germany.

Then came the last mile and the lieutenant laughed and said that from now on we'd be under observation by the Germans. There were two open fields to be crossed. The German shells had been dropping here all morning. There is a technique about crossing open fields at the front. The young lieutenant asks you whether the restaurants in Paris are still as good as ever. You light a cigarette and start walking casually across the field with him. And you tell him about the food in Paris. You start with the *pâté maison* at Pierre's, then touch on the fish at Armenonville and by the time you are discussing the small wild strawberries that Maxim serves you are safely across. Of course you're sweating a little.

Then finally you are at the last outpost. You go down into a large dugout and for a while watch the colonel in action. He has men at telephones and others with maps and he sits with his staff. His com-

mand has the fight of its life on its hands today.
Earlier in the day, prisoners had been captured. I
had talked to them. I had read instructions taken
from their pockets. "Stand fast," they read, "if you
retreat you will be court-martialed." The instructions were signed, "Your Fuehrer." Yes, the colonel
had a fight on his hands. He knew that 15,000 men
had been ordered to break through his lines or else.
But he didn't seem worried.

"How long you been here?" Pierre asked me suddenly.

"Four days and four nights."

"You like it?" André asked.

Like it? That wasn't a tough question to answer.
At this moment I wouldn't have been anywhere else
in the world. I wasn't with the army, I was in front
of the army. A month ago I was listening to Eddy
Duchin and loving it; I was having a drink with my
colleagues at *Collier's* and loving that. I was worried
about Carl Hubbell's left arm and Mel Ott's legs.
Now? Now I was in a steel-and-concrete observation
post in No Man's Land, watching flashes from German guns a mile away, listening to the roar of French
guns in the rear. Like it? Hell, I loved it. Today the
front was mine.

"Le Boche," André said, and there was excitement
in his voice.

I never met a French Army man who ever referred
to the Germans as anything but *"le Boche."* They
never said Germans. I looked through the slit and the
woods seemed quiet. Then I looked up. It was a Mes-

serschmitt. That's a good plane. He was flying lazily
down our valley. By now this valley belonged to us.
He flew quite close to us and Pierre swore very in-
delicately in French. His right wing almost kissed
our side of the hill but, of course, he didn't know we
were there. He was up for reconnaissance. Then,
miraculously, two black specks appeared. I knew
where they had come from. I'd spent last night there
at that little lopsided ridiculous airdrome. Then they
weren't specks. They were French Moranes—small,
maneuverable ships. Nothing like the Messerschmitt.
But nothing is, except the English Hurricane and
Spitfire.

The Messerschmitt wheeled quickly. We watched
and the guns suddenly stopped. The three planes
wheeled all over the valley in front of us. Then one
of the French planes seemed to get tired. When
planes are shot they invariably blow up in a glorious
cloud of flame and smoke. It's always like that in the
movies, anyhow. Actually planes don't always die
spectacularly. They die slowly. The French plane
wobbled and then glided down happily in back of
us. It seemed to be well under control, but it was out
of the fight.

Now it was one against one. A Messerschmitt
against a Morane. The Messerschmitt dived at the
Morane and I held my breath. Eight hours ago I had
sat in a Morane.

"It is simple," the pilot explained. "You hold the
wheel with your left hand. When the Boche gets
within the circle of your arm, your right hand presses

this button on the dashboard. Simple? That releases
your guns, 'Dop, dop, dop.' "

That's what the pilot of that little Morane was
doing now. Within two minutes one of these pilots
would be dead. It isn't fun seeing men killed. I see
men killed quite often, now, but it's hard to get accustomed to it.

The experts could tell you the maneuvers. The
Messerschmitt was above the Morane and then suddenly the little French plane raised its nose in the
air. He raised his nose and gained altitude and suddenly he was on top of the Messerschmitt. Pierre
grabbed my arm. I realized suddenly that my mouth
was dry, and that the neckband of my shirt was too
small. I've seen all the great fighters of our time but
I never saw anyone like this anonymous French pilot.
He was up against superior speed, superior arma-
ment, superior maneuverability. And yet he wasn't
getting hurt.

Then suddenly the Messerschmitt wheeled sharply
to the right and passed perhaps within two hundred
yards of our little nest. And the Morane was a hundred yards behind him. The Morane was firing. I
couldn't see the lead but I could see smoke trailing
from the wings. They hit something. The pilot? I
don't know. You aim for the pilot now in air fights.
His motor is armored too well. Shoot off half his
tail and he can still hobble to the ground; aim for
the pilot.

I think the pilot was hit. The Messerschmitt wobbled questioningly, uncertainly, and then dropped

rather slowly into the woods a mile away, the woods which hid the German battery that had been sending shells at that farmhouse all day.

It was very quiet, the guns of both sides hadn't resumed and, ridiculously, birds were singing protestingly above us. There was a phone at Pierre's elbow. Every ten minutes he had talked into the phone. He had usually said, in French, "Nothing to report."

Now he said it again. He was talking to a dugout two miles back. "Nothing to mention, everything is quiet, Captain." He was right, of course. Only a reporter who didn't know any better would be tense and excited at what he had seen these past few hours.

My escorting lieutenant had appeared from somewhere. We said good-bye to Pierre and André and started back. It was a long walk and then the darkness fell like a quick, black blanket. It began to rain; slow, miserable rain. There was no path to guide us. Now and then one of us would slip and more than once we ran into barbed wire. But we couldn't show a light, couldn't even smoke. Finally we got to a small village where troops were quartered. We went into headquarters. A dozen officers sat around smoking. It had been a hard day for them. One of them grinned and said unexpectedly, *"On les aura."*

They all smiled and something came back to their faces. *"On les aura"* is an expression made famous by General Pétain during the last war. He was at Verdun and things were bad. He sent one three-word message to Paris: *"On les aura."* It means, "We will get them."

The men around me were smiling now. One found nothing but supreme confidence at the front. Defeatist talk was the theme song of the loafers in the Paris bars. You never heard that kind of talk from soldiers at the front. They knew they were in a tough war but they felt too that they were going to win—or die. You got to believe them. I did.

I walked outside into the night. The guns were roaring again but that is a sound that is unheard after a while. Like the sound of city street traffic, it is all part of the scene.

It was pitch-black, but now and then flashes from the guns would streak upward through the night to light it for a moment. Trucks were rumbling past. Through the blackness I could distinguish a white square on the side of each truck. Inside the white square there was a red cross. These trucks were going away from the front. They were all full. One truck stopped and there was incredibly the sound of swearing in an unmistakable American voice. This was one of a group of ambulances belonging to the American field service. One after another they passed ghostlike through the night. There were a lot of them. They told the story of what had happened. It had been a tough day.

CHAPTER FOUR

THE WOUNDED DON'T CRY . . .

BOB MONTGOMERY had come over to join a group
of Americans who were driving ambulances. Downs
and I were back in Paris again trying to think up a
new excuse to get to the front. Meanwhile the three
of us ate at Maxim's and at Pierre's and the war
seemed quite far away. Nearly every day we'd drop
into the American Embassy to see the Military Attaché, Colonel Fuller, the smartest military man I
ever met. Gradually the red pins on his war map
were coming closer to Paris. The débâcle of Sedan
and Abbeville had come and gone. We even survived
the horrible nightmare of Dunkirk. Just — we
thought—a temporary setback. They'd never take
Paris.

Colonel Fuller was the only man in Paris who
knew what was coming. He advised us to make plans
to get out. He told us "off the record" that the French
Army wouldn't even bother to defend Paris. We listened patiently and then went to the Crillon or the
Ritz bar and said cheerfully, "Fuller is a great guy

but he doesn't know what he's talking about." Of
course he was one hundred per cent right.

It was Montgomery who gave us the excuse of
getting to the front again. He was leaving for Beauvais to join his group. Why not stow away in his
ambulance? So we packed our knapsacks again and
we went off gaily, bouncing happily inside the brand-
new ambulance. It was a lot of fun—until we got to
Beauvais.

At first it is hard to watch men die, but after a
while you get quite accustomed to it. Actually they
make it easier for you because they die very quietly.
The wounded don't cry. In a way it is harder to
watch a city die. Beauvais was a middle-aged city
still in the prime of life and it died very gallantly
but not at all quietly. Perhaps the story of the life
and death of this city and of the manner in which it
was killed might be worth the telling.

It was an ordinary French city, proud of its beautiful cathedral and of its home for the aged. It boasted
a little, too, of a large school for boys which was on
top of a hill overlooking the city. The city was very
close to the front, so close that the wounded were
brought directly to it from the front.

Downs, Montgomery and I met the city at ten
o'clock one night. The city was very beautiful at
night but perhaps that was because nearly a third of
it was in flames. The Germans had been bombing
it all day and, quite by chance no doubt, they had
scored a direct hit on the home for the aged. They
had also scored a direct hit on a hospital in the center

of the town, which was unfortunate because the hospital had been full of badly wounded. The school for boys on top of the hill had been turned into a front-line hospital and the wounded were brought there.

Orders had been given for the ambulances to move the wounded out of this hospital to the railroad station. There was a train there to take the wounded south. Twenty American ambulances did the work. They worked nearly all night loading up, then in pitch darkness crawling down the winding road to the station and afterwards returning for more.

I stayed at the hospital. I went into the operating room and it was very busy. There were two surgeons and three operating tables. A surgeon would look at the wound and then nod to an assistant. The wounded man would be put on the table and an ether cone would be placed over his face. Then his clothes would be ripped off and the surgeons would work quickly, deftly. Each surgeon had three assistants who weren't doctors at all.

A French artilleryman was on the table waiting and he was smiling gently and talking very fast. "It was good. It was good." The captain caught my questioning eye and he smiled. "Ten to one we got. There were only a few of us with our seventy-fives. The tanks came at us and we fired and fired and we destroyed those tanks as fast as they came to us. Each of our seventy-fives got ten tanks before they got us. The general had said, 'Hold your place or die.'

We did. Only I am left, but each of us got ten tanks."

Then this captain raised his hand to his lips and kissed it. "I tasted Boche blood," he said quietly, and then he laughed much too loudly and repeated, "I tasted Boche blood." He kept laughing and the surgeon put a needle into the fleshy part of his arm and then the surgeon shook his head and motioned to the orderlies to take the captain off the table. It was a pity the surgeon couldn't have done anything for this man but the surgeon knew what he was doing.

Both surgeons had been doing this ten hours now and they looked tired. Everything about them was tired except their hands, which were quick and fine and sure. They had run out of rubber gloves and they worked barehanded, occasionally dipping their hands into a pail of disinfectant. This operating room had been a playroom when the hospital had been a school for boys. There were pictures painted on the wall.

They brought in a huge Senegalese. They lifted him to the table and his eyes glanced at the wall to his left. Mickey Mouse was playing on that wall and near him was Popeye the Sailor eating a can of spinach. I caught the eye of the big Senegalese and grinned and he grinned back. Then I looked down at his leg which the doctor was examining and I stopped grinning. It wasn't a pretty wound. It was just above the ankle. The surgeon felt the thigh and nodded. It was firm there. Then he took a pot of iodine and swabbed the man's thigh with it and at first I didn't understand. They started to tie the hands of the black man to the table and he didn't like that. They do that because often the wounded get delirious as they are getting the ether and they thrash their arms around. But he let down quietly enough and they put the ether cone on his face. Then the doctor reached for something and he held the man's thigh with one hand and I walked to the next table.

I stayed there an hour, and it wasn't morbid curiosity because no one in his right mind would be curious about the reactions of men in a first-line operating room. I was there because this was my trade. I mean my trade is to find out everything it is possible to find out about war.

One by one, men were brought in and then a little later brought out again and not once was there a sound in the room except for the crisp directions from the surgeons and, of course, the sound of the guns, if you count that as a sound.

I left when they brought two women in who had been hurt in the bombing of the home for the aged. Both were very old but neither said anything. The wounded don't cry, not even the civilian wounded. But I left.

Outside the night was heavy with darkness. Except, of course, for the flames from the burning part of the town. But that was half a mile away. The darkness partially hid hundreds of still forms lying on the ground in front of a long shed where the wounded were first brought.

I picked my way among them and went into the

shed. Three nurses and one doctor were there. There were eighty-four wounded soldiers lying on the floor, sitting on chairs, on benches, and there were three wounded women lying there too. The nurses were examining wounds, putting disinfectants on the wounds, bandaging them. They were very wonderful. They gave their patience and their skill in the same abundance to a dull-witted black Senegalese and to a handsome French captain. One of the nurses stopped for a breath and she told me proudly that she and the other two nurses were from Beauvais; had been born here, and would die here. I was getting a warm friendly feeling for this city. This after all is the story of the city and I mention the hospital and the wounded merely as incidents connected with the death of the city; symptoms perhaps of how it died and why.

The night was alive with small noises—the sounds of the ambulances coming in; the whispers of the stretcher bearers; the "Easy, boy, easy, you'll be all right" of the American ambulance drivers. Now and then they would have to wait a few minutes for a load and then I would have a smoke with Larry Morgan whom his pals called Man-Mountain Dean because of his black beard; with the ridiculously youthful-looking Jon Thorenson or with Carl Quigley or Dave Stetson or Montgomery or Jack James.

Peter Muir, in charge of the drivers, was everywhere at once giving directions. The boys whispered that he hadn't been to bed in four days.

Montgomery drove up. Picture audiences who

used to watch the dapper white-tied Montgomery wouldn't have recognized this untidy apparition with blood on his hands and with grease and dirt on his uniform.

"The train is about full," he said gloomily. "This'll be our last load. These poor devils will have to stay here."

I went down to the railroad station with the last load. The long train stood there looking ghostlike in the darkness. Perhaps two hundred soldiers were lying on the station platform waiting their turn. But there was only room for the most urgent cases. It was very quiet there at the station. Downs and I helped pull out the stretchers. Then we'd hand them into the cars. We unloaded three of the four from our ambulance.

"No more room," a man in the car said tersely.

"We'll find room," Jack James said simply. James is tall and hard. I walked through the cars with him. Each one was filled. There wasn't an inch of room left on the train. We had to bring our lone casualty back up the winding road to the hill top. I sat in the front with Montgomery and James.

James said, "I haven't the nerve to tell him."

He and Montgomery looked at me. "He'd never understand my French," I said.

Montgomery took a deep breath, lit a cigarette and climbed down from the ambulance. He put the cigarette between the boy's lips and said, "There's another train in a few hours, kid. Don't worry . . . you'll be all right."

We drove back to the camp the boys had made under a large shed that had recently sheltered horses. The night was just beginning to get tired of it all and there was a glimmer of gray in the East. We sat under the shed on straw and drank whiskey and muddy water and it was good. Some of the boys flopped down on the straw and went right to sleep. I wish we could have taken the stretchers out of the ambulances and slept on them but the stretchers were full of rather horrible reminders of the many wounded who had lain in them today and even at the front it is silly not to consider infection. It's bad enough being killed by a shell or a bomb—who wants to be killed by a bug?

I had been at or near the front with the French Army for some time now and it was exciting to be with Americans again. We talked of colleges we had been to and of football and of a man named Roosevelt. One of the Boston men said, "Tonight I'd slug anyone who made a crack about Roosevelt." I liked that and I took out a pack of American cigarettes I'd been hoarding and gave it to him. I regretted it later and maybe sometime I can get it back from the President.

We were on a hill and from it we could see the city dying. The light from the flames was dull now because the dawn was thinning it out, so we slept after a fashion, but in an hour a man blew three notes on a bugle and that woke us. In this city that was the *"alerte."* That meant German planes are coming.

We walked sleepily out from under the shed and into the open field. It was bright daylight although it was only five-thirty. We heard the drone of the planes and knew without looking up that these were the two-motored Dornier bombers. But we looked up. There were only six of them flying in their familiar triangle with the odd two following the base of the triangle. We yawned. This hadn't been worth waking up for. But then we saw another formation of six following and another and another. . . .

They weren't high. They started dropping bombs. They were big bombs. We lay down in the fields, for there were no ditches, no holes to get into. We lay there looking at them. A few anti-aircraft guns began to bark foolishly. The planes came over us. The bombs dropped close to us. They made a heavy noise and you shook your head to clear it of the concussion.

"There's a hundred of them," someone called from behind a bush.

"I count one hundred and twenty," someone else said.

The bombs fell and whistled loudly and then exploded and you wished you were somewhere else. They were falling on our city. Thank God that one train had pulled out! The bombs kept falling forever. Five minutes can be forever. Then the planes disappeared into the sun. They hadn't been interrupted once.

Someone made coffee. We all felt tired now. A French artilleryman who had been manning an anti-aircraft gun in the next field came over for coffee. He had strong glasses with him. He had counted one hundred and twenty-six. That's a lot of planes.

Jack James said, "Anyone who says he isn't scared up here is either a liar or a damn fool."

We all nodded agreement. It was nice to know that James had been scared a little. He was the best of us, we all felt, tough, hard-working and with the gentleness of big, tough men. Once he said that he had been scared, we all felt better and we could lift our filled coffee cups without spilling more than a few drops. The planes came back three times within the next two hours. The tension drained us of vitality. In disgust James and Larry Morgan and Fuller pulled straw over them and went back to sleep.

Now a lazy column of black smoke came up from our city. Our city had been given its death blow and we knew it. It could never be proud of its lovely cathedral again. Its few small factories were smoldering sullenly.

Two hours after the planes had left for the last time there were three dull explosions. The planes had dropped delayed-action bombs. That's bad, because the ambulance men go into wreckage as soon as the planes leave, trying to save some people, and the thought that these time bombs may be lurking underneath a destroyed wall makes you work very quickly and sometimes you can't work as efficiently. Mind you, it doesn't prevent them from going into the buildings which are still hotly writhing in their death agony, but it forces them to work too quickly.

Edwin Watts was hurt by one of these. He was in a building when a delayed bomb exploded near by. The wall of the house began to totter and somehow Watts braced himself against the wall and held it upright until the injured were gotten out. He wasn't badly hurt.

Orders came from somewhere for us to leave the dying city. We wanted to ask questions: What of the boy we couldn't get on the train last night? What of that smiling nurse who had said she was born in the city and would die in it? What of the big Senegalese? We had orders to get out.

That meant that there was nothing the boys could do. They and their twenty ambulances had to move back a few miles. They hated to leave this city because they had come to love it and if that seems silly maybe we all get a little silly hearing guns all the time and watching bombers drop death encased in steel containers. Silly or not, it is true. I hated to leave it and didn't have the excuse the ambulance drivers had. They thought they could still do something. I was a parasite, watching things, giving nothing, helping none. But I hated to leave this dying city.

A soldier came to the camp and said that the Colonel in charge wanted to see Downs and me. His headquarters was in an old château, spotlessly clean. We stood in front of him like two schoolboys caught playing hookey. We knew that we had no right being this far up, and he knew that we knew it.

"You'll have to report to the General in charge of

this part of the army," he said. "It is a rule. You have no right to be here. The Deuxième Bureau has phoned me and given me orders. Proceed immediately to Lyons-la-Forêt and report to the General."

We said we couldn't leave; we had no means of transportation.

"You can walk," he said abruptly. "It's only forty kilometers."

I pointed to what was probably the healthiest ankle in France.

"*Mais, mon Colonel,* the ankle, you can see . . ."

The Colonel expressed sympathy and he smiled with his tired gray-blue eyes and said, "I will arrange transportation."

He gave us a car and a driver but after we'd gone a while we asked the driver to stop. We wanted to take another look at this little city. It was dying, all right. Those four ugly columns of black smoke were thick now. Mind you, in the military sense, the loss of this little city meant nothing. There were no munition factories here. It wasn't any kind of military base. It was just a small, insignificant French city that fate had tossed into the path of the ruthless god of war. Its death did not help the German cause in the slightest.

We watched it burn for a little while and then told the driver to get on. It was a pretty silent ride. It may be that those American ambulance drivers had so flavored the city with their presence that for us it had become a part of our country. All I can say is that it was mighty tough to watch it die and some day

I'd like to meet those who killed it. I'd like to have
Downs and James and Morgan and Thorenson and
Montgomery and the rest of them with me. Yes, that
would be nice.

We drove on and then the driver asked us if we
had a map. He didn't quite know where Lyons-la-
Forêt was. We had a map and we found that we were
on the right road. Then we hurried on. It was
strangely peaceful. The blue sky was herringboned
with ripples of fleecy clouds. To the right we could
hear the French guns.

"Listen to the echo of them from the left, Ken,"
I said. "There must be mountains off there and the
sound hits the mountains and bounces back."

We approached a small village and we asked the
driver to stop at a bistro. We wanted cold beer. It
was warm; we hadn't slept all night; we were thirsty.
We stopped at the one bistro the town had and to our
surprise it was closed. We drove around the town
and found it deserted. It had been completely evacuated. It gave one an eerie feeling to be walking
around a lovely town like this without hearing a
sound. We drove on a bit faster now. None of us
knew why but all three of us—even the soldier driving—were a bit worried. Some nameless small fear
seemed to be riding with us. We didn't pass a car;
didn't see a plane, a tank or an ammunition wagon.
The absence of life was uncanny. Then after nearly
an hour we reached Lyons-la-Forêt, a lovely secluded
village half hidden by heavy trees. We drove to headquarters. The General wasn't in but his aide-de-camp

was. He looked puzzled when we said we had driven from Beauvais.

"What road did you take?" he asked.

I showed him our map with the road penciled. He looked startled, then he threw back his head and roared with laughter. Downs and I looked at one another wondering what it was all about.

"You drove all the way through. . . ." Here the aide-de-camp broke down with laughter.

"Through what?" I asked.

"Through No Man's Land," he managed to choke out.

Downs and I felt ourselves getting pale. No wonder we had felt a strange tension. No wonder the village through which we passed was evacuated.

"I guess those weren't echoes we heard," Downs said. "Will you join us in a drink, *mon Capitaine?* I think after that the drinks should be on us."

(Note to Ken Downs—Still we had a lot of fun that day, Ken, didn't we? Remember that grand Bordeaux we had at the Captain's mess? Remember the ride back to Paris—ninety miles in ninety minutes? Remember how envious the rest of them were when we walked into the Ritz bar and told them where we'd been and what stories we'd gotten? It was fun working with you, Ken. We must do it again some time.)

CHAPTER FIVE

AND SO PARIS DIED . . .

THERE WAS NO DAWN.

This was puzzling at first because it had been a clear night. Now the air was heavy with a smoky fog so thick that you could reach out and grab a piece of it in your hand. When you let it go your hand was full of soot. Then you realized that this was a man-made fog, a smoke screen thrown over Paris to hide the railroad stations from the bombers. But for the first time in its history Paris had no dawn.

The restaurants and the hotels were all closed. For nearly a week there had been no way of hearing from or communicating with the outside world. A reporter without means of communication is a jockey without a horse. No matter what story you wrote now, you would be its only reader. And now the Germans were pounding on the gates of Paris. Already their mechanized forces had encircled the city on three sides. Within a day the thing that couldn't happen was inevitably going to happen. They would be in Paris.

It was time to say farewell to Paris. Virtually

everyone else had left. The Government had left. The cable office and the wireless had moved south. With the exception of a few newspapermen who had been assigned to the deathwatch the entire press had left. They had to leave. They had to follow their communications. Hotels were closed. There were no telephones, and not a taxicab on the streets. Today Paris was a lonely old lady completely exhausted. The last of the refugees were leaving, some on bicycles, some on foot, pushing overladen handcarts.

I had stayed behind to write the story of the siege of Paris, confident that the army would hold out in the north. Now it developed that there would be no siege of Paris. A lonely old lady was not a military necessity. She was to be reluctantly abandoned. The problem of how to leave Paris was solved by one of those incredible bits of luck that come only to fools who have waited too long. The Grand Boulevard was almost deserted this morning. One middle-aged woman was sitting at a table at a sidewalk café, one of the very few where one could still get coffee and bread. She was telling a few bystanders of her plight. She had driven into the city that morning in her small one-seated car. She had the car and two hundred francs, that was all. She would stay in Paris but she needed money. With money one could buy food even from Germans. She wanted to sell her car. Sell her car? For weeks people had been combing Paris, looking for cars. Offering fantastic prices, offering anything for means of leaving when the time came. I bought the car on the spot. She gave me the key,

I gave her five hundred dollars, which left me with five. No signing of papers, no transferring of ownership. I don't know her name yet, but I had the car.

Now I was mobile. Now I, too, could follow the Government, follow the wireless and the cable offices. My car was a Baby Austin, no bigger than a minute. Its tank was full of gasoline, enough to carry me a few hundred miles. There was room in it for a knapsack, a mattress, a typewriter and a steel helmet. And so the tiny car and I said farewell to Paris and headed south.

We didn't catch up with the great army of refugees until we passed the city limits. From then on we were a member of this army. It is one thing to see thousands of weary refugees in the newsreels; it is something quite different to be one of them. We moved slowly, sometimes we would be held up for as long as three hours without moving. The road stretched from Paris to Bordeaux four hundred miles away and it was packed solid that entire distance. Thousands of these people had come from the north, many had been on the road for two weeks. They had only one thought: move south. Move away from terror that swooped down from the skies. Move away from the serfdom that would be theirs under German rule. Few had any money. Few knew where they were going.

Some rode in open trucks and large, open wagons drawn by horses. Inevitably the sides of these would be buttressed by mattresses. These were not for sleeping. These were protection against machine-gun bullets. Refugees coming from Belgium and from Holland and refugees who had come from the north had been machine-gunned by Messerschmitts not once or twice but repeatedly. This is not rumor; it is fact.

Thousands in our army of refugees rode bicycles and they made the best time. Often a military convoy came down the road against our tide of traffic. Then we would stop and wait interminably until it passed. Those on bicycles managed to keep going, winding in and out of the massed traffic.

Thousands were walking, many carrying huge packs on their shoulders. This was a quiet, patient army. There was little talk. The hours passed slowly. My uniform and military pass gave me priority. And yet in eight hours I had only covered fifty miles.

It started to rain as night fell. Now we began to be held up by trucks and automobiles that had run out of gasoline. There was no gasoline to be had. Women stood on the roadside crying to us for gasoline as we passed. We could only look ahead and drive on. The rain continued to fall softly and the night grew very dark, which made us breathe easier. Even German bombers can't see through a pall of blackness.

Individuals would emerge from the mass when we stopped. Here on the roadside was a woman lying asleep. Her head pillowed on her bicycle. Here was a farm wagon that had broken down. A man and woman with their three children, the youngest in the mother's arms, looked at the wreck. The rear axle had broken and when the wagon collapsed its weight had completely smashed one wheel. They stood there looking at it, their faces empty of everything but despair. The road was completely jammed now. A man went from car to car asking: "Is my wife there? She has lost her mind. She has lost her mind."

He asked me and I said: "No, she isn't here." And he looked his amazement at hearing his mother tongue. He was English, had owned a bookstore in Paris. We heard a strange laugh and he ran toward it quickly. I followed. He had found his wife. She had left their car and now she had returned to it. She kept laughing.

Their car had run out of gasoline. They had no food. The woman laughed and then cried a little and said, "Help us."

I took the man back to my tiny car. I showed him my gasoline meter. I had less than three gallons left. There was no room in my car for anything. I had no food, I couldn't help. People around us looked on, saying nothing. There was nothing to be said. Thousands were in the same predicament. But this woman had cried. That was breaking the rule a little bit. No one else was crying.

Our army went on through the night. Hours later a whisper ran back: *"Alerte . . . alerte."* It had started perhaps miles ahead and had come back to us. The very few cars that had been showing lights snapped them off. Boche bombers were somewhere overhead in that black, unknown world above us. We were very quiet, thousands of us. I stepped out of my car. I flashed my light once to see where we were. I was in the middle of a bridge. Not a good place to be with German bombers overhead. But there was no place to go.

We stood on the bridge, kept from going either backward or forward by the press of cars and trucks and wagons and bicycles and people and by the blackness of the night. Far to the right we could see occasional flashes and now and then hear the sound of the guns. Faintly now we heard the hum of a plane. It may have been the drone of fifty planes, flying high. It's hard to tell at night. Then it stopped. It may have been a French plane or fifty French planes.

Our army resumed its weary, tragic march. Now some turned off the road. We were in a beautiful part of France. It was raining too hard to sleep in the fields that bordered the road. I drove as long as I could but the intense blackness of night strains your eyes as effectively as strong light does and when I had gone off the road twice I gave up.

Occasionally a car crawled by or a silent bicyclist or a few on foot passed. From the thousands and thousands ahead and behind came an overwhelming silence that somehow had the effect of terrific, overpowering noise. This silent symphony of despair never stopped. It was impossible to sleep. We sat in our cars and our wagons and waited for the dawn. It took hours for it to come and when it arrived it was a murky dawn. Without food or drink, we set forth south, always south.

We passed through small towns. Streams of cars

half a mile long would be lined up at a gasoline
pump that had run dry days before. Now we passed
stranded cars every few minutes. Sometimes people
pushed their cars, hoping that there would be fuel
in the next town. There was no fuel in the next town.
There was no fuel and there was no food. We were
the stragglers in this army. For more than a week it
had been passing this road.

At one town we passed a railroad station. A long
freight train was just pulling in from Paris. The
doors of the freight cars were open and humanity
poured out, spilled, overflowed. These were the cars
on which the famous sign, "Forty men, eight horses,"
was scrawled during the past war. Forty men. There
were at least one hundred men and women and
children in each of these freight cars. At each station the doors were opened for five minutes. This
train had been on the road nearly three days from
Paris. Once the train had been machine-gunned. Not
one, but everyone I spoke to, told me the same story.
It had been machine-gunned by eight German
planes. French fighters had come and driven them
off. Had anyone been hit? No one knew.

The congestion increased the farther south we
went. People looked even wearier. Thousands of
them had walked from Paris. We were a hundred
and fifty miles from there now. Finally I arrived
at Tours.

There was no rest for weary wanderers in Tours.
The bombers came, aiming for an airport on the
outskirts of the city and for a bridge that led south.

The huge square in front of the city hall was packed with tired refugees. They ran when the bombs crashed. When bombs fall close to you, your only thought is to get somewhere else. They ran but their heavy feet rebelled and when they fell they lay where they had fallen, shapeless bundles of apathy and despair. Three times within an hour the Germans came and the horrible, shrill noise of tearing silk that the bombs made as they screamed earthward and the shattering explosions a second later drained whatever small vitality there was left in the pain-racked bodies of these miserable children of ill fortune.

They had to move on. They stumbled on south, bearing the cross of their despair with the same courage and stoicism with which another had borne a cross nearly two thousand years ago.

Ken Downs and his International News Service crew had arrived in Tours three days before. There wasn't a hotel room to be had or a pint of gasoline to be bought in the city. I unrolled my sleeping bag on the floor in one of Downs' rooms in the drab Hôtel de l'Univers. I had a story to send so I hurried to the Town Hall where the Ministry of Information and the censor had set up offices. So had the incredible Louis Huat who was in charge of Press Wireless. Most of us sent our stories via Press Wireless. It was cheaper than the other services and then we knew that somehow Louis would get them through. I saw him work fifty hours in Tours without a break and not one complaint ever came from

New York about the condition of our stories when they arrived.

I brought my story in to the censor. He was a Colonel and new to me. He sat behind an untidy desk. I gave him my story.

"I'm very anxious to get this right off," I told him.

"Parlez français s'il vous plaît," he said curtly.

"Est-ce que vous n'êtes pas le censeur pour la presse américaine?" I asked in amazement.

"Oui, oui," he said sharply, *"je ne parle pas l'anglais mais je peux le lire."*

I winced at this and wondered again about that thin red line of red tape. I was beginning to remember everything that Colonel Fuller had said in Paris. This man was a censor—ergo—he could censor any copy. It was typically beautiful illogical French logic. What if he didn't know English? He was the censor, wasn't he? I sat down in front of him, much to his annoyance, while he read the story. It's a trick I've always used. I find (it's true even in London where I am now) that a censor hesitates to use his blue pencil if you are sitting right next to him. Anyhow it worked on this non-English-speaking Colonel.

He got to the last page, stamped it, nodded, said, *"Bon,"* and handed it back to me. I doubt if he had understood twenty words of it. I rushed across the hall to Louis Huat's office. He was there. When I handed him my story I knew that it was in New York. We all had the most fantastic confidence in Louis—none of which was misplaced. As long as

Press Wireless operated we'd all stay in Tours. It wasn't comfortable, but for the moment it was the news center of the world.

I went back to the bar of the Univers. Bob Casey of the Chicago *Daily News* was there. It was Casey who managed to write grand stuff all during the dull months of the "phoney war" which ended on May 10th. All winter long Casey sent beautiful stories to his newspaper. In our craft we have a lot of respect for Casey. He looks like a fat leprechaun who has lost most of his hair—but he writes like an angel.

"I picked him," Casey was telling the bartender. "The only one in Philadelphia to pick him."

"What did you pick, Bob?" I asked him after telling the bartender to give me a drink on Casey's bill.

"I picked Tunney to beat Dempsey in their first fight," Casey said stoutly. "And I bet on Tunney. The only one who picked him to win and who bet on him."

"I know another guy who picked him, sweetheart," I told Bob.

"Who?" Bob asked truculently.

"A guy named Gene Tunney," I told him gently. "Then there was another named Bernie Gimbel and a man you never heard of named Jack La Gorce, editor of the *National Geographic* and Ed Van Every, who is now with the *Sun,* and. . . ."

The scream of the siren interrupted me. I defy

anyone, even Hitler or Coughlin, to speak above the Tours siren. It sounded like a dentist's drill that had been wired for sound. There were about five women in the bar and six or seven men. We all stiffened a little. You do, you know. You can't be casual about a bombing any more than you can about a wedding. Whether you like it or not it's one of the biggest things that'll ever happen to you.

The bombs were landing close. Too close. The bartender ran from behind his bar. There were three large windows in the bar facing a courtyard. The bartender hurriedly closed the windows.

"That'll keep 'em out, pal," I told the bartender. He smiled happily.

"In the last war I used to be with the artillery," Casey said mildly. "We learned about a thing they call 'concussion.' If your windows are open and a bomb falls close, there is a good chance that the windows won't even break."

"Don't tell the kid, Bob, it'll only make him unhappy."

Bob and I had another drink—of course it was a whiskeyless day and we had to drink champagne orange, which strangely enough is half champagne and half orange juice. The explosions were near enough to make us wince at every crack, but they didn't bother Casey. Casey has a supreme belief in two things—his wife and his luck. Take him all around and Casey is quite a hunk of man. In our trade I never heard anyone say a mean thing about Casey and that's quite a tribute.

Ken Downs came running in with a rumor that there was a gas station less than five blocks away which had just been given a consignment of gasoline. I had about a pint of gasoline left in my baby car which was sulking outside the hotel. I practically leaped into it and headed for this oasis. When I got there I found a line ahead of me. I counted the cars. There were thirty-nine. I was the fortieth. I stayed there two hours getting nearer to the sacred font every little while. By the time I reach the gas pump there were at least a hundred cars behind me.

"I'm afraid there is none left." The buxom woman who ran the place was sweatingly turning the pump.

But she put the end of the hose in my gas tank and of course there was some left. Each of us was only allowed ten litres—that's about two gallons—enough to take me sixty miles in my little pushcart. There were just ten litres left. She pulled the hose out and shrugged her shoulders.

"And that, my pretty one, is what we call Reynolds luck," I told her. She didn't know what I was talking about but I did. I was mobile again. I could go halfway to Bordeaux, if I had to.

No one slept much that night. Rumors crawled around the streets of Tours like cats chasing their own tails. Sometimes the rumors caught up with themselves. Paris had fallen. Paris hadn't fallen. America had come into the war. America hadn't come into the war. It was like that all night and not much fun. All night long we heard German bombers flying over us. We actually thought it was a tough night. I'm glad we couldn't see ahead. I'm writing this in London in my lovely apartment. The only drawback is the fact that two hours ago a bomb landed across the street and knocked all of my windows out again—the third time. Yes, there must have been a dozen German bombers up over Tours that night. Tonight there are probably four hundred over London. But we'll let that pass. Let's get back to Tours.

The next morning I went to the good old Town Hall first thing to see good old Louis Huat, to see if my message had gone through. It had gone through. I went into the censor's room once more. The censors weren't there but the painters were. Then a horrible and incredible rumor swept through the building. The Government had left secretly at five A.M. for Bordeaux. The Government hadn't told anyone. Tours was useless now. Louis Huat, his eyes bloodshot, a four-day beard on his tired face, said, "I'll get to Bordeaux somehow. I'll be ready for you boys when you get there."

The painters kept on painting. I told them that the Government, the censors, the Ministry of Information, the wireless, had all moved or were about to move to Bordeaux so why in hell were they keeping on with their painting. They kept solemnly stroking the dingy walls of the room with nice oyster-white paint.

"We got orders two weeks ago to paint the inside of this building," one of them said. "Government orders. So we're going to finish the job."

"I hope Dr. Goebbels will like it," I said and left. It was as good an exit line as any.

CHAPTER SIX

BORDEAUX WAS CROWDED ...

DOWNS, KNICKERBOCKER AND I held a council of war. We decided to evacuate Tours—but immediately. By now we knew enough about the Blitzkrieg tactics of the Germans to make plausible the rumor that kept leaping from pub to pub, that they were on the way to Tours. If we were caught in Tours it wouldn't have been good for any of us. Knick and I were on their black list. Downs had been accredited to the French Army. Even if they didn't kick us around they would make us immobile. They certainly wouldn't let us file stories. And then there was the fairly well substantiated rumor to the effect that Bill Bullitt had told friends that America would be in the war within eight days. If America came in we would be enemy aliens. It seemed the better part of valor to run like hell. We ran.

It was dark when we left and the German bombers were chipping away at the city. We decided to spend the night at the Château de Cande, which was the headquarters of that portion of the American Em-

bassy which had been sent out of Paris. It was a
lovely estate. It was here that Mrs. Simpson had
married her silly English lover. Or, to put it the
other way: it was here that the Duke of Windsor had
married that silly American woman. Never were so
many thousands of words cabled about less, as were
cabled about the solemnizing of that holy union.
When they die, on their tombstone should be en-
graved, "They Deserved Each Other."

But it was a lovely estate. The outer gate was
locked. We rang and rang, and finally an ancient
bundle of plumpness arrived to ask sharply what we
wanted. Downs had covered the Simpson-Windsor
imbroglio and she remembered him. He told her
what we wanted—room on the lawn to sleep. She
grumbled that she'd have to get permission from the
American Embassy which occupied the house. She
went away and didn't return. We were in no mood to
dicker. We'd all had a tough seven days and we
wanted a night's sleep. Knick and Downs climbed the
iron picket fence and walked the mile and a half to
the house. They aroused a sleepy and very junior
member of the Embassy staff. Reluctantly he came
back with them and opened the gate.

He brought us to the stables and said that we could
have all the blankets we wished. We were a bit put
out, because our relations with the Embassy had been
excellent. We had been accustomed to the effusive
friendliness of Ambassador Bullitt, the genial com-
panionship of Maynard Barnes, the press attaché,
and of Colonel Fuller. Any of them would have said,

"Here's the house, boys. Come in, have a drink, and make yourselves at home." But this very junior member was very sleepy and not at all interested. So we took the blankets and rolled up in our sleeping bags on the closely cropped lawn sanctified by the fact that once it had been trod upon by the high-heeled shoes of La Belle Simpson. However, happily none of us heard those aristocratic footsteps and we all slept as comfortably as one can sleep on a dew-wet lawn.

The sun woke us early and we decided to ask the junior member of the Embassy for a few gallons of gasoline. We threw pebbles against the high windows of the lovely house. No one awoke. There was of course only one thing to do. We went to the garage, found a short length of hose and siphoned a few liters of gasoline from the Embassy cars which were standing there. We comforted ourselves with the excuse that had Bullitt been there he would have given us all the gasoline we needed. Afterwards in Bordeaux we met some of the American Embassy lads who told us that the theft of the gasoline had made the junior members of the staff very angry. Our replies were more vigorous than polite. I still know that Bullitt would have said, "Come in, boys, the place is yours. Gasoline? Take all you want." Junior members of an Embassy are apt to take themselves more seriously than do their bosses.

And so we headed for Bordeaux. Mickey Wilson had planned a route that took us by way of back roads. We had the roads entirely to ourselves and it was for the moment grand fun. Now and then we'd find a bistro open and we'd gorge ourselves with bread, cheese and wine. Then we'd push on. My Baby Austin never faltered. And in small villages we found gasoline pumps which gave us all the fuel we needed.

Then we arrived at chaos and Bordeaux. The incredible Louis Huat had set up offices in a large loft building. It had been a labor union headquarters and it was all concrete and steel. The censor was here and what was left of the Ministry of Information. We found a large empty office and put "Official" on the door. This was our home. We unrolled our sleeping bags, put our typewriters on desks and did everything but put drapes on the windows. Bordeaux was normally a city of 250,000 people. Now there were three million of us in the city. Bordeaux was bulging at the seams. Bordeaux was an overfilled sack of flour tied too tightly around the middle. It was night and thousands were standing in front of restaurants. When they were told that there was no food left they continued to stand there. Wild rumors chased one another along the dark, packed streets. The Cabinet had resigned; Reynaud was out; there was talk of capitulation. Added to the pain and misery stamped, perhaps permanently, on the faces of these homeless, there was now bewilderment. This thing couldn't be. This country their ancestors had built could not die. They and their fathers before them had tilled the soil, had nursed vineyards and had watched green leaves grow into sturdy vines and had seen the wonder of grapes being born and living and growing. Then they had turned the grapes into pure wine.

What crime had they committed that they should now lie miserably in fields and in city streets? Had they placed too much faith in their rulers?

I sat in a crowded restaurant. The *alerte* sounded. Lights were put out and service ended. A trembling voice cried: "Fifty Boche planes are coming over Bordeaux. I heard it. I know it is true. Fifty planes will kill us all." The voice came from the woman who ran the restaurant. No one moved. No one said anything. We were all a little bit embarrassed for the woman. Then an officer laughed. "Stop talking nonsense, Madame. Go back to your kitchen and find fifty eggs. We are all hungry." The woman stared ahead for a moment, brushed the hair back from her forehead and turned into the kitchen. The night was soft, trying perhaps to make one forget the helpless misery of three million homeless who were on the streets of Bordeaux. But no one looked up. The magic of the night was ignored. People were too tired. The English journalists hurried to a ship that had been sent for them. They had to get out quickly. We Americans were safe enough for the moment. We crawled into loft buildings to sleep. It was easy to sleep even on hard floors. The flight from Paris had been a long one and a tiring one.

In the morning the homeless again started their pathetic trek to the south. Many left cars on the streets. There was no gasoline. Many abandoned broken wagons and cars and smashed bicycles. Where were they going? They didn't know. For days and for weeks they had endured this agony. It was not a pleasant sight to watch, this twentieth-century Gethsemane.

Then came the incredible rumor, quickly verified, that the Reynaud Cabinet was out; that Pétain was in. People clutching at straws of hope, cheered wildly. Pétain and Weygand would run things. Two tough army generals—they'd stem the tide of defeat. Pétain, the hero of Verdun—he'd rally the army.

Sitting in the darkness of our loft building retreat, Downs and I weren't so sure. Neither was Knick, or a couple of French correspondents whom we knew.

"Foch was always the man of action," one of them said cautiously. "Pétain was his assistant. Pétain was the careful calculating one. Foch was the strong one. Foch and Clemenceau. Pétain is a strategist . . . but wait."

We didn't have long to wait. The next day Pétain made his incredible speech of capitulation which sickened us all. He called upon the army to stop fighting. We knew that Winston Churchill had come to Bordeaux and promised Pétain a division a day if he'd hold out a bit longer. We knew that Bullitt had talked to Pétain and had told him that America would help in every way.

That day Downs and I had lunch in the Chapon Fin, one of the world's finest restaurants. I think that only Horchers in Berlin and the Colony in New York compare with it. We only got in by showing our military passes. It was an incredible gathering. Pierre Laval was at one table gnawing on his moustache. Keen-looking Georges Mandel was at the other end of the room looking tense and white. Genial Anthony Drexel Biddle was at another table, urbane, smiling, jocular, although he was under a terrific strain. Parenthetically it might be added that he, deputizing for Bullitt, did a magnificent job getting American and English refugees out of Bordeaux.

France was falling to bits around our heads, but Downs could talk solemnly to the wine steward about what kind of Bordeaux we should have with our hors d'œuvres; what kind of Burgundy with our meat. And for the moment that was the most important thing in the world to the *sommelier*. And of course to us. We hadn't slept in a bed for a week and we hadn't had a bath. Our uniforms were filthy—but we had Nuits-Saint-Georges, 1923, and we had sole Marguery, and after that steak with a wine sauce. And then Napoléon brandy—that probably really was Napoléon brandy.

"The condemned man ate a hearty meal," Downs said happily.

"I wish we were condemned to this for a month," I said.

Mandel arose and walked by Laval's table without saying a word to him. A French newspaperman Downs and I knew, stopped Mandel and talked briefly to him. When Mandel went out, our French colleague came and sat with us.

"What did Mandel say?" I asked him.

"He said, 'If my name were Du Pont I could still save France. But it is Mandel.'"

It was a rather horrible statement, but of course

true. Mandel was magnificent. He was a protégé of Clemenceau. They called Mandel the Tiger's Cub. He was one lone voice crying aloud in the wilderness but even his fine honest voice could not be heard above the rustle of red tape; above the clink of gold that found its way to the pockets of the men in power; above the confused babbling of incoherent minds.

Mandel will soon be dead, I suppose. The Germans would be fools to let him live. As long as there is breath in his body, Mandel will go on screaming to his people to fight. Mandel had only two faults which prevented him from controlling the Cabinet. He loved his country too much to be a clever politician and he was unlucky enough to have been born in the faith of Jesus.

That was a bitter night in Bordeaux. People finally realized that it was all over. As dusk fell, Downs and I sat at a table outside a café. We felt as bad as the thousands of weary refugees who passed ghost-like in the gloom. Now and then we heard mutterings as people noticed the "American War Correspondent" on the shoulders of our uniforms. America had promised so much—and had done so little. Speeches by prominent Americans promising help for France had been printed every day in the papers. The French people were foolish enough to have believed them. There were a few soldiers now passing, a little drunk, filled with despair and hatred and disgust. It was hard to blame them.

"We'd better get out of these uniforms," Downs said quietly.

I agreed. We climbed into my ridiculous car and went to our loft building. It loomed large and dark and deserted-looking. Practically everyone had left. We climbed the stairs wearily.

"I'm not very proud of being an American tonight, Ken," I said.

"I'm not either." Downs had been stationed in Paris for several years. He'd gotten to love the country and the people. We sat on the floor of our dreary office not saying anything much. We felt as if we were attending a wake. I fumbled around on the desk and found a bottle of wine and half a loaf of bread. We ate the bread and passed the bottle back and forth and tried to rationalize what had happened.

Why did France collapse? By now everyone has written about that, and given reasons. André Maurois in his excellent articles in *Collier's*, "What Happened to France," told the story. Downs and I that night could think of but two reasons why France was now dead. First of all there was the Maginot Line. That extended, you'll remember, from the Swiss frontier to Montmédy; that is, to the Belgian frontier. At first it was proposed to build the line right through to the sea. King Leopold of Belgium, however, suggested mildly that he would consider it an unfriendly act if the Ligne Maginot were built along the French-Belgian border. Brave Belgium would be barrier enough if an invader were to come. The French believed it. The biggest and most costly white elephant in history stood there blinking in the sun while the fighting all went on miles away. Had the

Maginot Line been extended to the sea there would have been no Sedan, no Abbeville, no Dunkirk.

And then Mandel's name was not Du Pont!

That's what Downs and I decided that night in Bordeaux, sitting on the floor in the darkness, drinking wine and eating stale bread. Nothing that has happened since has altered our opinion. We decided another thing that night. We decided to get the hell out of Bordeaux. The next day we did.

CHAPTER SEVEN

I GAVE HIM DOUBLE TALK ...

AND NOW WE'RE RIGHT BACK where we started from, on the dock at Pointe de Graves. Downs and I had heard that a Dutch freighter was to leave for England from Pointe de Graves. We got passes from the Embassy which entitled us to a passage on the ship. Then we headed for the harbor. Reluctantly I left my Baby Austin in front of the Café Suisse in Bordeaux, hoping that someone would provide it with a good home. It had been a friendly little car.

Downs decided to evacuate his whole staff to England. Mickey Wilson had gone two days before with Knick and the English newspaper men. But we still had a formidable group to get on that ship. There was Merrill Mueller, John McVane and his wife, Lucy, William the office boy and the Comtesse Jacqueline de Moduit. Jackie was the office secretary. She was French of course and she had worked for Downs for several years. A few days before she had left Paris she received news that her husband and her brother were both "missing." Jackie bore up

beautifully Convinced that both were dead and that
France too was dead, she wanted to go to England.
But she had no passport. We couldn't get her a pass
to board the freighter. However, she decided to drive
from Bordeaux to Pointe de Graves with us.

We all slept on the dock or in the fields adjacent,
waiting for the dawn. It was a long time coming.
Then a brisk English naval officer appeared on the
scene. He was in charge of getting refugees out to the
ships.

"You are all going on the S.S. *Benekom,*" he said.
"The ship is supposed to wait for a train load of
people coming from Bordeaux but I have a suspicion
that the captain may get the wind up and just leave.
I'd better get you out there now."

He had a tender waiting at the end of the dock.
Downs handed him the key of his car.

"It's almost new. I can't take it with me," he said.
"Maybe you can find a use for it."

The officer shook his head wearily. "I've been offered two hundred cars in the past week. Sorry, I
have no use for a car."

Downs asked him if he wanted our passes. He
shook his head impatiently. Obviously he didn't want
to be bothered with any red tape. Jacqueline stood
there looking at Downs. Ken tried to look away. We
all stood there awkwardly. We had all been through
a lot together and the thought of leaving Jacqueline
alone in France made us all miserable. However, she
had no passport, no pass for the ship, and legally had
no right to leave France. But Downs was the boss.

"Come on, Jackie," he said, and for the first time in a week, Jackie smiled.

We climbed into the tender. The dawn was just beginning to come over the horizon. The *Benekom* was a sturdy, ten-thousand-ton freighter, and she looked awfully good to us. The Chief Engineer met us as we climbed aboard. He was all smiles and he spoke English. He verified what the British naval officer had said. The captain was getting a bit worried. During the night the Germans had dropped bombs all around the ship but had missed. Then they had returned and swooped low and had machine-gunned the *Benekom*. The captain would be very happy to get to sea. There was hot coffee waiting for us in the galley, the Chief added.

A tarpaulin had been spread over the aft hatch, and this was to be our home. We unrolled our sleeping bags and unpacked. We had been told that each of us could bring aboard only what could be carried in a knapsack. I had two bottles of brandy, two cans of tongue, a toilet kit, a half dozen handkerchiefs and my typewriter. Downs had about the same.

"This is going to be a difficult trip, *mon Général,*" I suggested to Downs. "We'd better start working angles right now."

We always called Downs "The General." He had a genius for organization. The fact that his whole staff was here on board proved that.

"I'm the General," he said a little wearily. "I only function on land. How about you being the Admiral? What angles can we work?"

"I will love up the Chief Engineer," I said. "A Chief Engineer always has a nice cabin. Somehow or other we have to end up with that cabin of his. Then we have no cigarettes—none at all. Maybe he has some. I'll start by giving him a bottle of brandy."

I went to the Chief and asked his permission to look at the engine room. I told him that I'd been to sea for years and had always worked in the engine room. Actually I had made one trip as a wiper on the *K. I. Luckenbach* when I was sixteen. But the Chief's face lighted up. He was proud of his engine room, as well he might have been. I admired everything I saw. Then he offered me a cigarette. I almost swooned when I saw what it was. It was a Chesterfield. I hadn't had one since leaving Paris. I practically forced the bottle of brandy on him. He protested weakly and then suggested that we drop into his cabin for a drink. It was just six A.M. No man ever had more of a fuss made over him than that poor engineer. I lit his cigarette. I poured him drinks. His cabin was roomy and very comfortable. Finally he asked me shyly if I'd like to look at a picture of his wife and children, and then I knew I had him hooked. I squeezed a crocodile tear out of my eye when I saw the picture of his fat, healthy-looking children.

"That girl is so lovely. My little one had she lived. ..." I couldn't go on.

"Ah yes," the Chief said, putting his arm on my shoulder. "It is like that. I know how it is."

"My pal Ken Downs would love to see this picture," I said, sprinkling my voice with a dash of Hearts and Flowers. "He has two children just about the same age."

"Would he join us in a drink?"

"I'll get him," I said, and practically ran to the hatch. General Downs was testing out the sleeping possibilities of the hatch.

"Awfully hard," he said. "I don't think we'll get much sleep here."

"The Admiral would like to report that the Chief Engineer is well in hand," I told him. "Come along and see our new cabin."

"Is the Chief giving us his cabin?" Downs asked.

"He doesn't know it yet, but he is," I said and brought Ken in to meet my man. Downs went into proper rapture over the picture of the youngsters. I thought he overdid it a bit when he said that the Chief's wife reminded him a little bit of Myrna Loy, but the Chief lapped it up. I thought it was time to really get down to business.

"Chief, I'd give anything for another one of your cigarettes," I said. He opened a drawer and there, lying on top of shirts and socks, were two cartons of Chesterfields.

"My God," Downs breathed.

"Looks like we struck oil, pal," I muttered to him. The Chief gave us each a pack of cigarettes. Within a half hour he had dug up a cabin for Lucy McVane and Jacqueline. We, of course, could use his cabin any time we wished. Just make it our home, he said. It wouldn't be such a bad trip after all, we decided.

We walked out on deck feeling pretty well satisfied with ourselves. It was one of those south of France mornings. Once upon a time Scott Fitzgerald wrote a book called *Tender Is The Night*. It was about the south of France. He described those incredible mornings. For a description of this particular morning, pick up *Tender Is The Night*. I reread that book once every year. It was like that this morning, soft as the neck of a kitten.

Then we had a rude interruption. Fifty yards from the ship a geyser of water shot into the air to the accompaniment of sound effects. It was one of the loudest explosions I'd heard up to that time. The big ship swayed gently, the geyser fell slowly, the water bubbled angrily—and then everything was silent. This was a magnetic mine. The bombers had dropped it during the night. It had fallen between our ship and another large freighter lying perhaps two hundred yards away from us. Apparently the steel attraction from both ships was fairly equal, so that the mine couldn't make up its mind which way to go. It must have spent a miserable night shifting back and forth. Then its frustration found outlet in its own destruction. I found I was sweating a little.

Then we heard the buzz of airplanes. We couldn't see them at first, and then we discovered a dozen of them, silver white, flying high. Red Mueller had joined us at the rail and we kept looking at the planes which seemed to be directly headed for us. What were they? Then Mueller said, "It's all right. They are French Moranes."

We relaxed. Mueller was the only one of us who knew about airplanes. In addition to being a fine reporter, Red was a fine pilot. If he said they were Moranes, they were Moranes. At that time I couldn't tell a Flying Fortress from an Autogyro. Since then Goering has educated us in London. Now we listen for a moment, don't even bother looking up, and say blithely, "There's a Boulton Defiant on half throttle." Of course we are practically never right, but we think we are. There is only one infallible test to determine whether a plane above is a German or an English bomber; stand there and if it drops a bomb on you, then you are fairly safe in assuming that it is a German plane.

The little Moranes flew over us and why they didn't keep right on flying to England I don't know. They'd come in handy these days. But they didn't. Then somewhere aft we heard a heavy grating noise; the anchor was being lifted.

The Chief Engineer came out and said, "Yes, the Captain has had enough. We are off."

"Well, we've had a hell of a farewell party," I said.

"I will be on duty for the next four hours," the Chief said. "If you care to take a nap in my cabin. . . ."

Downs and I were in a sleeping mood. We couldn't remember when we'd had a decent night's sleep. We crawled into the Chief's bunks and if the harbor was full of floating mines and if the sea outside was infested with submarines, they'd have to function without our help. We slept.

The trip from Pointe de Graves to Falmouth was very dull, which pleased us enormously. There were only thirty-five of us on board so there was enough food for us all. It was pretty dreary food and we had potatoes and soup twice every day, but even that didn't bother us. It was quiet. The reaction of the past few weeks had set in and we were all a bit nervous and irritable. We needed a rest and we got it. We even peeled potatoes every morning and liked that. I was excused when the cook discovered me absentmindedly saving the skins and throwing the potatoes away. Jacqueline and Lucy McVane, who should have been miserable and unhappy at the rather difficult cramped quarters and dull food, were the brightest of us all. The war has shown us one thing; women can take a beating much better than men can. The two girls had even miraculously made their hair attractive. Two great troupers—those girls.

Twice during the trip we were told that submarines were in the vicinity. But we were bored with bombs and with guns and with killing, and we yawned, stretched out on the hatch and slept. The Chief Engineer's cigarettes held out and the ship's store yielded six bottles of sherry. It had nothing else, but we were happy with the comfortable cabin belonging to the Chief and the Chief's cigarettes. Then one morning we sighted land. The trip had taken four days. Because we were alone and unconvoyed, our Captain had done a lot of zig-zagging, which made the trip much longer than it would have been ordinarily. Falmouth harbor looked mighty nice to us. It was filled with ships—we counted ninety-five. Many were refugee ships, others freighters from South Africa or Australia. They were battered-looking ships, dingy in their war paint. Most of them had the white line painted around their hull showing that they had been De Gaussed—made immune to magnetic mines.

We hoped that we could get off that day but no one came from shore. No one came the next morning either and we began to think that we were a forgotten ship. Downs and I went into a huddle. We decided to send a wireless message to Joe Kennedy asking him to facilitate our landing. We wrote a nice long cable, but then found that the ship's operator could not send it. It was forbidden to send messages while in port.

That afternoon a launch drew up alongside. Two naval officers, looking mighty smart, climbed aboard. They looked at the ship's papers and then cheerfully told us that we probably would have to wait another day or two.

"Falmouth is crowded with refugees," they told us. "The dock is packed with people who have been waiting twenty-four hours just to get into town. Then the line at the customhouse is half a mile long. You may as well stay here."

Between us we managed to scrape up ten dollars. By that I mean that Downs and I managed to get a ten-dollar bill which Red Mueller had been hoarding. We gave that to one of the naval officers with our cable. He sent it and the next morning a boat came to take us off. It was a dreary, rainy day, the first rain we'd seen in weeks. The boat tied up alongside. A couple of officers scrambled up the side. We all leaned over the rail looking down below at the tidy little craft, at the Union Jack flying proudly from it. A grizzled old sailor looked up at us. We were a dreary-looking crew, Dutch, Belgian, English refugees and our Americans. Refugees as a class are the most unattractive-looking people in the world. But the old sailor smiled and waved a cheery hello to us.

"There'll always be an England," he shouted up complacently.

We thought our troubles were over now. We realized that we had been over-optimistic when the tender brought us to the dock. It was a big dock, perhaps seventy yards long. It was absolutely packed with a seething, miserable mass of men, women and children. There were at least three thousand on the dock. There was an iron gate at the shore end of the dock. Every fifteen minutes or so they let ten refugees through. At this rate we'd be here for eight or ten hours at least. The rain had increased. There was no shed over the dock. There was no place to sit down.

Then came a cheery voice calling for the "American journalists." It was from a messenger from the Foreign Office. Joe Kennedy had really gone to work.

"The Foreign Office instructed me to get you right through," the messenger said, and we breathed hap-

pily again. We gathered our knapsacks and our typewriters and our messenger, escorted by a policeman,
led us through the envious but apathetic crowd.
Finally we reached the iron gate which was guarded
by a huge Sergeant.

"I have a message from the Foreign Office to let
these American journalists right through," our messenger said importantly.

"Well," the Sergeant smiled, "if you'll just show
me the message I'll let them through."

"The message was phoned from London," our man
said. "I haven't it in writing."

"Sorry," the Sergeant said briskly. "I have my
orders. Every one takes his turn unless there are
written orders."

We stood there, soaking wet in body and mind.
Freedom was only a step away and this obdurate sergeant was blocking it. The messenger argued loudly
but ineffectively. There was nothing to do but to go
back to the end of the dock. It was getting dark now
and the rain had increased. Everything else having
failed, I thought as a last resort I'd try something.

"Sergeant," I said, speaking low and confidentially.
"If I could explain perhaps you'd understand. We
don't want any special privileges, in fact we wouldn't
accept them even, but in Bordeaux the English Ambassador called us in and asked us if we would hurry
to England. He put us on a special boat," (here I
lowered my voice and the Sergeant, attentive at least,
bent an ear) "and we must get to Fleet Street because
Winston Churchill wants us but it's confidential and

I know you won't after all." (Here I raised it) "What the Foreign Office wants us to do I don't know, but Duff Cooper cabled us to, as soon as landed, well, he wants and I suppose it's some sort of propaganda as Winston Churchill says," (here my voice trailed right off the dock but I looked him straight in the eye) "well, you know the pornus is strictly a thing and you can't go around talking branf about sarong and Mr. Churchill. God knows we don't" (good and loud) "want special privileges but if Mr. Churchill . . . you see how it is."

The Sergeant nodded thoughtfully, "In that case, of course," he said heartily, "anything at all. Go right through, gentlemen. You'll find a taxi right down there."

We walked proudly down the dock. Downs, Mueller, McVane, the two girls and William the office boy were looking at me with awe. We got into the taxicab. The Foreign Office messenger was with us.

Downs said, "What the hell did you tell that cop? I couldn't understand a word you said."

"That, my pet," I told Downs, "is what we call double talk. It doesn't mean a thing. It wasn't a very good example," I said modestly, "because I had to improvise very quickly. But I have learned under the masters. Eddie Moran and Charlie Butterworth and John McClain and John O'Hara in Hollywood; Milton Berle and Mark Hanna and Jimmy Cannon in New York. Thank them, my lads, for having gotten us through."

"That's probably the first time," Red Mueller said, "that double talk ever took the place of passports."

"Now, we'll see how it works at the customhouse. Remember Jacqueline and William have no passports."

William was the son of an English father and a French mother. Although he had been born in France he was technically a fifteen-year-old British subject. His mother was dead and his father was somewhere in Switzerland. He was just another one of Ken's responsibilities. It would be difficult to prove to the custom officials that William was English. The only English he knew was a phrase I had taught him "Nuts to you, sweetheart." I told him that was English for "Merci."

"Warn the kid not to answer any questions when we get in there," I told Ken. Ken did and the kid grinned and said, "Nuts to you, sweetheart," and looked at me for approbation.

"*Bon,* William, *bon,*" I told him.

"If you'd stop giving English lessons maybe we'd get to London without being arrested," Downs said.

The custom people proved very tractable. Just a dash of Eddie Moran double; a few plaintive bleats about the trials and tribulations we'd been through; a few airy references to Joe Kennedy, Duff Cooper, Lord Beaverbrook and Winston Churchill and we each had a little slip giving us uninterrupted passage to London. We were officially labelled "refugees" and as such could change our French money into pounds at the excellent rate of 176 francs to the pound, almost normal exchange.

"Where," I asked one of the custom men, "could we put up for the night?"

He looked us over thoughtfully, "You'd be most at home at a pub called the White Hart down by the docks. Yes, that's about the best place in town."

It was too late to get a train to London so we tiredly got back into two cabs and headed for the White Hart. But I hadn't liked the way that custom man had said, "You'd be most at home at the White Hart." I asked the cab-driver what it was like.

"A good rough and ready place," he said. "It's used mostly by the dock workers."

"I'd like to go back and slug that custom guy, Ken," I was storming.

"Maybe if we could take a good look at ourselves," Downs said drily, "we'd understand what he meant. Remember, we've been living in these clothes for many a day."

The driver told us that the best hotel in town was the Falmouth. We headed for there. It was a large, sprawling wooden building with a tidy lawn stretching down to the water. The lawn was dotted with blue and white flowers. It looked too good to be true. We walked in and, almost trembling, asked for rooms. They had plenty of rooms if we didn't mind doubling up.

Ken and I doubled up in an enormous room complete with bath. We pulled back the covers of the beds and fingered the beautiful white snowy sheets.

We tossed to see who would bathe first. I won. We began to peel off our clothes. They were cracked and muddy. Downs, the General again, now that we were on land, stalked briskly to the phone and ordered a bottle of Scotch and another of soda. I dove into the bathtub which was about the size of Billy Rose's Aquacade pool. I lay back and stretched and went right under the hot water. I hated even to put my head out.

The waiter came. Ken fixed a drink and brought it to me. Mind you I would have done the same for him but I had won the toss. He looked with distaste at the water. It had gradually assumed a dull, gray color.

"Ken, I promise never to darken your bathtub again," I said. "Give me that drink."

I lay back again, the water steaming and the Scotch and soda cold. Without any doubt I'll always remember that as the happiest moment of my life.

I yelled in to Downs, "Ken, I want to ask you a very important question."

"What is it?" he said.

"What can heaven have that we haven't got here right now?"

Downs thought awhile and then he called back, "No typewriters."

Lenoir Rhyne College
LIBRARY

CHAPTER EIGHT

THEY CALL HIM REVOLVING
REYNOLDS . . .

BUGS BAER ONCE SAID, "All towns outside of New
York are Bridgeport." I used to agree with Bugs that
once you left New York you were strictly on the
horse and buggy circuit. But of late years I've had
to modify that. Since then I've discovered New
Orleans and San Francisco and a little place called
Carrizozo, New Mexico, where I want to go when
I die. I want to go there and hang around the drug-
store and sneak behind the prescription counter with
Art Rolland and have a nip of what he calls Old
Granddaddy and then type out his prescriptions for
him. I want to eat the Mexican food that Sadie Rolland cooks and play "high-low-jack-and-the-game"
with Tom and Belle James and with Art and Mad-
eline Kudner and with our mob from the Oh-Bar-Oh
Ranch. I want to talk baseball with a rancher, Big
Whit, who takes care of the bar at the Carrizozo
Country Club. He's such a baseball fan that he uses
a baseball for his brand. I want to sit around arguing

with Art Kudner, taking the opposite side of any
argument just to draw Art out and listen to him talk.
Carrizozo seems a long way off from Berkeley
Square where I'm writing this to the accompaniment
of a lot of noise. If I could have New York, New
Orleans, San Francisco and Carrizozo I'd be willing
to let the Indians have the rest of America. I can
never be neutral about cities—I like them or I don't
like them.

And I like London. A city is as good as the men
you know in the city. Girls are pretty much the same
in every city and in every country, but men aren't.
I've always known grand people in London and perhaps because of that I overrate the city and give it
a charm that it actually lacks. I've been in London
a dozen times and I feel as much at home in London
as I do in New York. I've never been in Westminster
Abbey but I know every pub in Fleet Street. I've
never visited the Tower but I could get a job on any
paper in London. I never saw the changing of the
guard at the Palace but I've often sat with Frank
Owen, the editor of the *Standard,* and have heard
him argue magnificently with Arthur Christiansen,
editor of the *Express.* I've never gone to Kew in lilac
time but I know Bevin and Beaverbrook well. I've
never punted on the Thames but I can find my way
from the Strand to Berkeley Square on the darkest
of blacked-out nights. I know London as a newspaper
man knows it and that's the best way to know any
city.

I know it as Ed Beattie of the United Press knows

it; as Tommy Watson of INS knows it; as Bill Stoneman of the *Chicago Daily News* knows it; as Chris and Frank Owen and Paul Holt and Hannen Swaffer and Valentine Castlerosse know it—and when you know London like that, why it's only a larger Carizzozo. It's just as friendly. I like London.

When we arrived from France, London was a bit panicky. For years the dreary Conservative party had been telling the people that everything was just dandy. But now Dunkirk had come and gone. Only incredible courage, amazing luck, and unexpected German stupidity had saved the English army from complete annihilation.

We thought the invasion would come any day. It will always be a mystery why Hitler allowed England to catch her breath. If he had followed Dunkirk with an invasion he would now be eating his carrots and beets in the Dorchester or the Savoy. Last July a fight between the German Army, supported by its then magnificent air force, and England would have been a fight between Joe Louis and Joe Doakes. Even the War Office admits that now. But unaccountably Hitler held back. He had all of the British tanks, guns, food supplies, even tobacco, which were left behind. Recently German airmen who were captured were found smoking Players. They had come from the immense stores left in France by the retreating army.

A lot of us think that England won the war at Dunkirk. She lost about 35,000 men. She should have lost 350,000 men. Nothing as bad as Dunkirk ever happened to an army before. I can't say much about it because I wasn't there and I think a man is a fool to write "think" pieces these days. But I have spoken to at least twenty service men who escaped from there and to the captains of both trawlers and motor torpedo boats which helped bring the men back and from them I got a pretty good picture of what hell it must have been.

To begin with the huge army which waited on the beach had virtually no anti-aircraft guns. The German bombers had a real field day. It was like shooting fish in a barrel. The army just sat there taking its beating. Eventually the English fighting planes came to drive the bombers off but they didn't come for some time.

When they did come they didn't stay long. Hurricanes and Spitfires carry fuel enough for about an hour and a half of cruising. When they have to dive sharply and zoom upward at full throttle and go through their other tricks that hour and a half becomes about an hour. So they were no great help.

Why the whole force of the Luftwaffe wasn't hurled at those men on the beaches until they were all killed is one of the major mysteries of the war. Why Hitler and Goering who have (from a military standpoint) been so magnificently decisive should have chosen that moment to split a herring or sing "Horst Wessel" or take part in a barn dance no one will probably ever know. A month later it was too late.

The best minds in Fleet Street thought that Hitler

would move into Ireland. So did people at the War Office. So many Air Ministry and Admiralty figures told me "off the record" that Ireland was to be next that I began to believe it. It seemed logical. Germany would have as much trouble grabbing Ireland from De Valera as Wallace Beery would have had snatching a peppermint stick from Shirley Temple. I hated to leave London. London was calm now and peaceful and we were beginning to say, "He'll never bomb London." It was just wishful thinking but for the moment we all believed it. Then I found that smart Ed Angley of the *Herald Tribune* had sent a man to Dublin; Ray Daniels of the *New York Times* had sent someone over; Chris had hurried a man to Ireland; Bob Low of *Liberty Magazine* was on his way; so was brilliant Virginia Cowles of the *Sunday Times*.

It was time I left. I went the next day. I'd never been to Ireland before. My idea of Ireland was Donn Byrne and James Stevens and *Portrait of the Artist as a Young Man* and *The Dubliners* and *I Was Walking Down Sackville Street*. I spent two weeks in Ireland and didn't find any of the things which I had found in those books.

Vincent Sheean was in Dublin. He had left London a week before, intending to sail for New York on the *Washington* which was making its famous last trip. But Sheean (who has never been called anything but Jimmy) changed his mind at the last moment. He stayed on in Dublin trying to get an interview with De Valera.

Parenthetically I did get an interview with De Valera. It wasn't very successful. First I found that I'd have to share the interview with Bob Low. I liked Bob but I like to work alone too. But it was the only way to see the head of Ireland, so reluctantly I went along with him. Gallagher, his press attaché, told us just before we went into Dev's office that the interview was strictly "off the record." That was just ducky. I didn't want to meet Dev socially—I wanted to ask him questions—the answers to which I could print. I tried to back out of even meeting him but Gallagher pleaded.

"He's anxious to see you," he said. "He wants to know what it was like in France."

So Bob and I went in and met the tall, homely, sad-eyed man and within five minutes his charm had completely captivated us. If Dev had a beard he'd look like Raymond Massey, who looks like Abraham Lincoln. He was anxious to hear about the German tanks and about the German parachutists—but he was talking "off the record." You get to respect that "off the record" tag. You can violate it only once in our business. It gets around if you do.

When we left Low asked me what I thought of Dev.

"How the hell can I tell anything about him!" I stormed. "You never let him get a word in edgewise."

But to get back to Jimmy Sheean. Jimmy was once one of the best foreign correspondents in the world. Then he started to write books. He wrote *Personal History* and that was a hunk of writing. That was something for all of us to shoot at. I think that only Webb Miller (*I Found No Peace*) equaled it, and as far as the business of being a foreign correspondent went Webb Miller started where the rest of us left off.

Now Jimmy Sheean divides his time between reporting for the North American Newspaper Alliance (NANA) and writing books and plays. In Dublin he had a suite of rooms at the Shelbourne Hotel that you could have held a skeet shoot in. If you stood at one end of his living room on a clear day you could just see the other end of the room with the naked eye. But Jimmy had spent his honeymoon in this suite and so although he was alone this time he took it again. Low and I were also living at the Shelbourne so we could keep an eye on each other and we spent an evening with Jimmy.

Jimmy had been away from London for a week and he was anxious for news. The Irish papers were strictly censored and not much news crept into their moribund columns. I mentioned casually that the biggest news of the week was Knickerbocker's great beat on the seizure of the French fleet at Oran.

"He licked the world by four hours," I told Jimmy. "He got a great cable from Barry Faris and another from Joe Connolly. That's the biggest beat of the war."

"Where did he get the story?" Jimmy asked tersely.

"He was at a dinner party," I explained, "when Brendon Bracken came in and spilled it."

Brendon Bracken is Winston Churchill's Parliamentary Secretary.

"I was at that dinner party," Jimmy exploded. "I left it early and came here the next day. But Brendon didn't say we could use the story. I assumed that it was off the record. So I left the party and went home."

"But Duff Cooper was there, James," I reminded him softly. "Knick went to work on Duff after you left. Knick said that if the American press didn't hurry and give the English version of the seizure the German radio would have a garbled version ready for American consumption. Knick worked hard on Duff and persuaded him to release the story. And then Knick ran like hell to the censor with Duff's okay and got it through before anyone in England knew about it."

Jimmy got up, his face white. He poured a drink deliberately. He drank it. He sat down again.

"I had that story just as Knick had it," he said tensely, "but any time I get a story at a dinner party I figure it is off the record."

"When people ask Knick or you or me to dinner, Jimmy boy, they are on notice. They know how we make our living. They have no right to impose any implied 'off the record' edict on us."

Jimmy said thoughtfully, "I'm mad. Not at Knick. I'm mad at myself. Damn it all, I used to be a good reporter. What's happened to me?"

"You're not hungry any more, Jimmy," I said. "You've got to be hungry to be a good reporter.

Knick is hungry. Me? I'm starving. But you aren't hungry. You aren't hungry to see your by-line over an exclusive story. You don't get the same kick out of licking the rest of us that we all get out of licking each other. You've written too many books."

"You're right," Jimmy sighed. "My God, you're so right. I keep thinking of stories in terms of a book."

"Well, that's all right. You make more money than the rest of us put together. You have an easy life and you're pretty much your own boss. Most of the boys envy you, Jimmy."

"Do you?" he asked.

"Not me. I'm a reporter. You're a writer. I don't get any kick out of writing. I do out of covering a story."

We talked back and forth about it and Jimmy was still mad when Bob Low and I left. He was mad at himself. I hope he doesn't change his mental attitude and become what he once was—one of the best of all reporters. Competition is tough enough as it is.

I think that there is more good, accurate, honest reporting going on in England today than ever before in the history of our craft. To begin with the boys work under tough conditions. Most of them have to work at night. Then because we have no cabs in London at night they have to walk home. Walking a mile at three in the morning through black London streets with bombs falling and with shrapnel falling all over is not like having a waltz with Hedy Lamarr.

But they bear up magnificently. You laugh a little when you think of the men who made great reputations out of the last war and how little they had to endure to earn those reputations. To us one man has emerged from this war as the master of them all— Bill Stoneman of the *Chicago Daily News*. There is a newspaperman. The fact that he writes well is not important. Writing is just putting one word down after another as Damon Runyon once so aptly put it. But he runs his bureau efficiently. Of course he has a great staff with a brilliant girl, Helen Kirkpatrick, working for him. Bob Casey who was the head man in France for the *Chicago News* came over to help out afterwards. But in London we all think that Stoneman is the best of us all. I hope that the *Chicago News* bosses never discover his amazing honesty, integrity and ability. If they ever do they'll make an editor out of him and one of the greatest reporters who ever lived will be dead. I might add that this opinion of Stoneman is shared by every correspondent in London—and no one is jealous of him.

But to get back to Ireland. I wrote a story about Ireland for *Collier's*. I have a great-grandfather buried in County Donegal. I am sure if he read my story he turned over in his grave so many times that they now call him Revolving Reynolds.

CHAPTER NINE

THE IRISH DON'T BELIEVE IT

IT WAS BACK in 1922 when the Black and Tans finally turned their hated backs upon the shores of Ireland. The last boatload of them was just leaving when a stalwart Dubliner made a remark that has come to be part of the saga of the Emerald Isle.

"Thank the Lord they've gone," he said lustily. "Now, praise be, we can fight in peace."

Today Ireland is very unhappy at the thought of someone infringing upon her traditional heritage of fighting peacefully within her own borders and with no outsiders participating. Ireland is in the tragic position of being a likely battleground for two foreign nations—one nation that she hates and another to which she is indifferent. Ireland, beyond stoutly declaring her neutrality and streamlining her small army as well as she could, is solving the whole problem by blandly ignoring it.

"It is like this," a member of the Dail said to me earnestly. "If either of them invades us, by the living Lord we'll fight and kick them right out. If Germany invades us, why, we might allow England to help us kick them out. If England invades us, well, we've been fighting England for seven hundred years and know how to handle her."

I heard this in homes in Dublin and in pubs in Cork and in small village inns in Tipperary. I heard it in the eight-hundred-year-old palace of an earl, and in country clubs in County Wicklow, and again I heard it in Galway on the west coast. No matter what tall, anxious-looking De Valera says; no matter what the dour-looking William Cosgrave, leader of the Opposition, says; no matter what William Norton, leader of the Labor party, or what gentle, scholarly old President Douglas Hyde, say—that is the opinion of the people of Ireland and it is one thing on which they are absolutely united. Ireland is committed to neutrality and, by God, Ireland will stay neutral if it has to fight everyone in Europe to maintain its status. I heard this a thousand times in two weeks from the people of Ireland and I heard it whispered to me by Government officials talking "off the record."

Coming to Ireland after the nightmare and death of France and after the tension and horrible feeling of dreaded anticipation in London was like emerging from a dark, dank swamp into the brilliant light of the sun. You heard far less war talk in Dublin I am sure, than you do in New York. There were no black-outs and no soldiers on the streets. Prices were the same as they had always been and there was a heaping plate of golden butter on the breakfast table alongside a filled sugar bowl—two things that the eyes of this correspondent had not seen for many a long day.

There is a war going on but, praise be, it is no war of Ireland's. It is a war between England and Germany and the Devil take them both. That is the well-known ostrich defense used so ineffectively by Holland and Belgium, the two neutral twins who still don't know what hit them. If you stick your head in the sand these days the obvious thing is sure to happen. But Ireland shrugs her shoulders, looks at tomorrow's entries, and doesn't believe it.

I visited Glendalough, which is the vale between the two lakes in Wicklow. It has been a Sunday-afternoon picnicking ground for Dubliners for two hundred years. I was looking for likely places where the German parachutists might land. Glendalough is the place where in the year 504 Saint Kevin built his seven churches and then retired to a cave overlooking the lake. One night the fair Kathleen, in love with the fire of his eloquence, came to tell him of her love but the holy Kevin pushed her away, and down into the dark blue waters of the lake she went, never to come up again. Then Kevin in remorse decreed that never again would anyone drown in the lake and to this day none has.

There were probably two thousand laughing people from Dublin there, and they were telling the story of Kevin to solemn-eyed children, and they were having tea at the lovely inn on the shores of the lake, and to them the legend of 504 was far closer than the nightmare that has come to life in 1940. This is true: there in fact is the very cave and the ruins of the churches that the good saint built. Parachutists? Fifth columnists? Get on with ye, now.

For two weeks I looked in vain for just one man who was afraid of the potential invasion by the Germans. I never found him. I walked into the bar of the Royal Hibernian Hotel, and forty men were deep in form charts, figuring out possible winners at Phoenix Park. I ordered a Scotch and began talking to the bartender. The bartender winked at a man standing next to me and said to him, "This fellow is here for the invasion." "Never mind the invasion," the man said. "We'll take care of those blighters if they ever come here and mind that."

I went to the Elm Park Country Club just outside of Dublin. Here the fairly well off businessmen of Dublin meet each day to play golf and each night to drink and talk. The lawyers, the merchants, the newspaper editors, the automobile salesmen—it is a perfect cross section of substantial Dublin.

I knew them all and they laughed a little bit at me but tempered their laughter by taking me into their circle. Reggie Knight, prominent Dublin businessman, says, "Now what a pity we haven't a few little parachutists for you to play with tonight. But here's Michail Buckley from Cork. Men from Cork never open their mouths for fear that by mistake they'll order a round of drinks. And Jack Arigho, who played wing three-quarter on three Irish Rugby teams that beat England; and Norman McBratnea and Con Foley and Paddy Duffy and Larry O'Neill, and now, lads, there'll be no closing hour tonight."

Someone asked me about the German tanks and how they operate. I told him. He laughed and said, "Some of our lads with rifles could pick their eyes out."

"But this is not a war between men, but men and machines," I said desperately. "The parachutists land with machine guns and carry hand grenades in their belts and flame throwers that shoot a flame a hundred yards."

"Come now," venerable Lawrence O'Neill said soothingly. "Have a wee spot and forget your machines. Did you know that I went to school with James Joyce?"

Enemy planes over Ireland? Ridiculous—and what if they did come over? Ireland had planes.

Holland had planes and so did Belgium and so did France. How many planes did Ireland have? Well a dozen or so and fine little things they were. Oh, but you wanted to scream at these happy, lovable, charming people and tell them to wake up, destruction might be just around the corner. But they'd slap you on the back and Jack Arigho would go to the piano and play "The Minstrel Boy," and sing it in his high, sweet voice, and Pat O'Loughlin would make another speech of welcome in Gaelic which not a man in the room would understand, for only three per cent of the people of Eire know the mother tongue, more knew it until it became compulsory to learn and then, of course, none would study it any more.

If the civilian population of Eire laughs at the thought of invasion the military does not. In many ways the terrain of Ireland will be an ally if the invasion comes. There are only two real airports in Ireland. It is true that the plains of Meath and Kildare and of Tipperary would provide ideal landing places for enemy planes, but it is equally true that these meadows and moors are cupped or surrounded by high hills. Most of the coast is rocky, but there are several wide beaches not unlike the beaches on which the parachutists and troop-carrying planes landed in Holland. There is Portmarnock, near Dublin, which gleams whitely with what looks to be firm, hard sand. Kingsford-Smith once took off from here on a flight to America. So did Jim Mollison. But military authorities who, incidentally, cannot be quoted by name, say that the sand is soft in spots and that even the infallible Reed's *Nautical Almanac* cannot tell how high the unpredictable tides will come and how much sand will be firm on any given date. Incidentally, precautions have been taken to protect all of Ireland's beaches.

Ireland has a few potential naval bases well worth the attention of any invader. Germany would love to hold Cobh and Berehaven on the south coast; Lough Swilly on the north-west coast and Killary Harbor, which is in Galway. Also Bantry Bay in Cork and Dunlaoghaire in County Dublin. This

would give her a Gibraltar to keep a conquered
England in order.

It wasn't until the third week in July that Irish
ports were mined against invasion. Then Sean
Lemass, Minister of Supplies, speaking for the Government, said that the coast was being mined and that
the Government was gravely concerned about the
possibility of invasion. Dublin only yawned.

None except military authorities, who won't tell,
know just how large the Irish army is. In July, 1940,
it was roughly 20,000 men. Today, augmented by a
local defense force, it probably numbers 80,000 men,
but the latter are not trained soldiers. Under the command of Major General McKenna, it is organized to
fight the kind of defensive war that may develop.
Colonel Costello and Major General Hugo McNeill,
who learned his soldiering at the military school at
Fort Leavenworth, have organized the army into
brigades, not divisions. A brigade—perhaps a thousand men—will have everything that a division has
except man strength. It will have light artillery,
heavy artillery—what there is of it—tanks—what
there are of them—and, of course, infantry. It is a
compact, fast-moving unit which knows well the
terrain where it is stationed.

These brigades are strategically placed, each one
being responsible for a limited amount of territory.
If any belligerent forces land, the brigades will
theoretically be on the spot within a very short space
of time. The important roads have been mined and

there is no doubt that the Irish army will put up a sturdy and wholehearted defense.

If they come by air, using planes as a main attacking unit, the brigades will not be quite so effective. But military strategists still insist that no army can win a war from the air. They saw Germany conquer France through its planes, which were undoubtedly the deciding factor, but they still don't believe it. Military experts still insist that wars are won by infantry, ignoring the evidence that might be given by Poland, Norway, Holland, Belgium and France.

Once a group of bombers and dive bombers thoroughly strafe a section of country there is little opposition left. Then the parachutists by the hundred can descend in peace and quiet. This is not a military theory out of an antiquated army textbook, this is something I have seen happen myself. This is warfare of 1940.

If Germany decides to invade Ireland, she will probably do it by air. First her attacking planes would clear the ground; then a thousand parachutists would land; then the troop planes, each carrying forty men, would come down. Within an hour Germany could land three thousand well-equipped soldiers on any Irish airport. She will drop baby tanks from planes as the Russians did when they went into Rumania.

There are six small counties in the northeast of Ireland. This is the part of Ireland that still serves and belongs to England. There are English troops in Ulster. If the Germans strike and the Irish fight back, which, of course, they will, these English troops will automatically become allies of Eire. Ireland, without losing face and without taking one step backward from her announced policy of neutrality, will then allow England to come in to help repel the invaders. These are good soldiers, many of them veterans of Dunkirk. They are well-equipped with light tanks and armored trucks which could bring them along Ireland's fine roads to Dublin within two hours. They have planes there to protect the roads against the dive bombers and there are other planes waiting at Liverpool, only eighteen minutes away by air from Dublin. If Dev, as all of Ireland calls the unassuming, troubled Prime Minister, in the name of the people gives them the word, they won't linger. And it is possible that one of the major engagements of the war will then be fought on Irish soil.

The man in the pub doesn't see the picture that way at all. Neither does the man at the races or the squire getting ready for the next horse show. The 1940 war is very far away to him. Rather would he talk of the time in 1014 when the Dalcassians of County Clare drove the Danes out of Ireland. Rather would he talk of Michael Collins and of how back in 1920 when there was a price of 40,000 pounds on his head he would walk gaily along O'Connell Street every day, rubbing elbows with the Black and Tans.

These things are real to him.

To understand the Irish one must study them at long range. You cannot get to know them by living with them. You will get to know that they are lovable and honest and gay and very brave, but this is not understanding. They profess no love for the English but the huge, gilded statue of Queen Victoria, which is in front of Parliament, is still one of the show sights of Dublin. Eire is almost wholly Catholic, but today Douglas Hyde, the President of Ireland, is a Protestant. Ireland is intensely democratic but is very proud of its fine Royal Hibernian Hotel in Dublin. Ireland says, "We want nothing to do with England," and yet 95 per cent of her exports go to England. Ask an Irishman as I did to explain these paradoxes and he'll shake his head and smile. "Don't try to understand us," he'll say. "Hell, we don't even understand ourselves."

I'd had enough of Ireland. I went back to London. Then all of a sudden it was September 7th and the war really started. It's been going on ever since. Do you want to know about how things are in London? Things are like this ...

CHAPTER TEN

TIME OUT FOR GOSSIP . . .

THIS IS A VERY UNIMPORTANT CHAPTER which might well be omitted. It's just a chapter of random thoughts and gossip. The rules of rhetoric demand, if I remember rightly, unity, coherence, emphasis. All three are lacking in this chapter but perhaps the anecdotes and trivial incidents which you are now going to have the doubtful pleasure of reading may add up to something. They may serve to give a quick glimpse of what London is like today. When the war is over those of us who survive will be able to sit down and write quiet objective and undoubtedly boring books on what happened to London during her Gethsemane. But the agony is going on now—at this very minute bombs are dropping within a block of Berkeley Square where I live. What follows is gossip and stray bits of news about London today.

There is an office building on Bond Street just off Piccadilly. The doorman wears a uniform but it isn't a very resplendent uniform. The doorman at the Radio City Music Hall would shudder at its drabness and its shabbiness. The doorman too, looked very shopworn. He was about sixty and had a scraggly moustache. The only reason I noticed him at all was because of a rather peculiar incident. There was a general going in just ahead of me and when he saw the doorman he stopped, saluted briskly and then went into the building. I stopped to see what it was all about. Soon a couple of those glamour boys in their R.A.F. uniforms passed the building and they saluted very respectfully. Within ten minutes a dozen officers had gone by and each had saluted the old doorman. He returned their salutes carelessly, almost patronizingly. Then I noticed something I hadn't seen before. On the left breast of his uniform there was a small deep purple ribbon and on it lay a tiny bronze cross—the Victoria Cross.

Since 1856 only 1,102 V.C.'s have been awarded. The last two were awarded this month. So highly do the English think of a V.C. wearer that the ranking officers salute him even though he is a shabby doorman in a shabby uniform working in front of a shabby office building.

Maybe there is a moral in this. I don't know. But it is the kind of thing that could only happen in London. There is not a man or woman in England who isn't confident that the country will win the war. I have seen recent New York newspapers and the answer to this confidence is expressed by them in the thought, "The English are either very brave or very stupid." I think they are very brave.

God was very good to the English—He made each

one of them half a fool. An Englishman is fool enough to believe that one Englishman can lick a dozen Germans. The R.A.F. kids aren't boastful, but each one is foolish enough to believe that he and his Spitfire can lick a dozen Messerschmitts. Women and old men in the villages have built street barricades and they are foolish enough to think that they can defend their villages in case of invasion. The fact that each Englishman is half a fool gives him a tremendous psychological advantage over any German who is no fool at all, but instead is a reasoning methodical being who knows the rules and abides by them.

The Englishman is also foolish in this respect: he thinks that his personal liberty is the most important thing in the world. In New York if a cop orders us gruffly to move on, sheeplike we obey him. Here the Englishman will want to know why. If the cop has a good reason, well and good. This is reflected in the English newspapers which now I guess, are the only comparatively free newspapers in the world. Of course we have never had freedom of the press in America so we don't know much about it. Always our newspapers have been dominated by advertisers. No publisher will deny that. Here the editor of a paper means something. He actually writes almost as he pleases.

Last September the papers were full of vitriolic criticism of Duff Cooper. Duff had formed a sort of private Gestapo which went around questioning private citizens.

The papers really went to work on it. Here the editors write their own editorials. Percy Cudlipp, editor of the *Daily Herald,* blasted Duff's undercover men out of existence with a phrase. He called them Cooper's Snoopers. The others took up the cry.

Duff Cooper took and paid for big advertisements in the London papers defending his stand. · The papers in which his advertisements appeared attacked him the hardest. Frank Owen, editor of the *Evening Standard,* told his political writer Michael Foot to go to work on Duff. Michael Foot is to England what Heywood Broun was to America. Every time I read anything that Michael writes I get sick with envy and jealousy. Duff made a speech in the House attacking the "yellow press" for its criticism of his ministry.

Michael Foot wrote in the *Standard:* "Mr. Duff Cooper has no luck. He will discover this morning that his most vigorous opponent is *The Times,* whose vulgar and intrusive methods of inquiring into the more sordid aspects of human behaviour and whose strident methods of presenting news are so much deplored in Fleet Street and elsewhere."

Arthur Christiansen, editor of the *Daily Express,* coined two phrases which swept the country. He demanded that this be a People's War and that there be a People's army; that is, that all workers and ordinary civilians be armed and trained. Each day he screams against the brass hats in the Cabinet, the Army and the Navy. There won't be any Pétainism in this Cabinet with these editors keeping an eye on things. You see, in France the papers never criticized, never told the truth. No paper in France published the news of the fall of Paris until five days after the city fell. Things like that can't happen here.

Here's another thing the English have on the Germans and on us. They have a great sense of humor. If we want to criticize someone in public office we work up a terrific hate against him and use an ax for a weapon. The Englishman laughs him off.

The Home Guard offers many examples of the English sense of humor. There are one million seven hundred thousand men in the Home Guard now, most of them middle-aged or older. They are paid one and six (thirty cents) for standing watch. I was with a bunch of them the other night. The paymaster came around to give them their money. The first man in line was a rather dignified gentleman, about sixty. The paymaster handed him his one and six and said: "Now, sign here and then sign this paper and here's the third one."

"We have to sign in triplicate?" the man inquired politely. "Well now, that is interesting. I happen to be president of a bank. Every day I sign receipts for ten, twenty and sometimes fifty thousand pounds. And I never sign more than once. But then I suppose you know your business better than I do."

(P.S. A week later the Home Guard only had to sign one receipt.)

The soldiers have the greatest sense of humor of them all. Right after the hell of Dunkirk two old buddies who hadn't seen each other since the war began met in a pub. You'll remember that Wednesday was the worst day of all at Dunkirk.

One of the lads said to the other: " 'Ow was that Wednesday at Dunkirk?"

" 'Ow was it?" the other exploded. "Bloody awful. Rained the whole bloody day."

Sense of humor? I spent the last week end in the country and on Saturday night went to the local village pub. There is a regiment of soldiers stationed near and several of them were in the pub. They were celebrating the return of one of them. He had been in the military jail for ten days. It seemed that he had always longed to go to sea and here he was, as he said, "in the blarsted army in the country." So one day without even a leave of absence he walked to the nearest port and signed on a merchant ship as a sailor. Just told them he'd been discharged from the army. He took a five-day cruise with the ship and found that he didn't like the sea at all, so he returned to his regiment. He was promptly court-martialed.

"The Colonel, he asks me, 'And 'ow did ye like the sea?' " he explained. "So I says, 'Colonel, forgive the expression but the sea is no bloody good. I was seasick all the time.' "

The Colonel laughed and gave him ten days in jail. In the German or Italian army the man would have been shot for desertion.

The pub is the real birthplace of wit in England.

I walked into a small pub in London where I'd been several times before and noticed there was a new barmaid in charge. I got talking to the proprietor and asked him why it was he changed barmaids so frequently.

"It's like this," he said earnestly, "if the barmaids don't like me, then I fire 'em, see? And if the barmaids do like me, why, my old lady fires 'em."

I've spent a lot of time with the young fighting pilots at an airport near the Channel. They all wear life preservers when they fight over the Channel. Actually they are life jackets. They are rather plump in front and the boys call them their "Mae Wests." This started off as R.A.F. slang. But the higher-ups heard the expression and began using it. While I was at this airdrome an official notice from the Air Ministry was put on the bulletin board.

It began: "It has come to my attention that some pilots forget to put on their Mae Wests before taking off. In future remember never to take off without wearing your Mae West." It was signed by an Air Marshal.

One of the pilots of a Spitfire was reprimanded while I was there. The day before his plane had been hit in a fight over the Channel. He bailed out and floated in the Channel for three hours. Not a single ship spied him. Finally as darkness was falling an English destroyer passed close to him. He shouted frantically but no one on the destroyer heard him. Finally in desperation he took out his revolver (modern cartridges don't get water-soaked) and fired six shots at the bridge of the destroyer. The ship swung round, thinking a submarine was firing at it and saw the kid in the water. They lowered a boat and hauled him aboard. The captain was spluttering with rage.

"Those shots missed me by a foot," he roared. "I'm going to complain about this."

He did so. The kid's commanding officer reprimanded him officially in these well-chosen words: "Young man," he said sharply, "the Admiralty complains that you shot at a captain of a destroyer. In future do not waste your ammunition on captains in His Majesty's Service. That is all."

The incident was forgotten.

The other night German bombers came over the west coast dropping pamphlets giving the text of Hitler's last speech; a speech, incidentally, which was printed in every newspaper in England. In one enterprising village the pamphlets were collected and then auctioned off. The proceeds went to buy tobacco for the soldiers. How can you beat a people who use laughter as a weapon as the English do?

Who ever started that myth about the English having no sense of humor? The newspaper boys here display placards. The day the Italian ship *Colleoni* was sunk by the *Sydney* the newsboys outside my apartment had a placard reading "Wops lose Boat Race." Today there has been terrific fighting over the Channel. About noon the newsboy in the Strand (the newsboy is about sixty) had a placard announcing the results in football language. His placard read: "Only about 39 shot down. Extra period being played." I returned three hours later and under that he had written: "After extra period score now 69 to 8."

There are no holidays in England any more, no one wants a holiday. Even the Cabinet Ministers work. Yesterday I wanted to see Lord Beaverbrook. He asked me if I could meet him at one-thirty at his home. That is one-thirty A.M. When I arrived Beaverbrook was eating a steak.

"Have you had dinner?" he asked.

"I nearly always have dinner before one-thirty in the morning," I told him, with what I hoped was fine sarcasm.

"That must be nice," he said thoughtfully. "I seldom get around to it until about this time."

He's a very tough little man. We sat and talked for a couple of hours. What about? Damon Runyon. The Beaver is a great admirer and pal of Damon's. Beaverbrook is a combination of Knudsen and La Guardia.

I've been down in the Channel villages when they've been bombed. In France people used to freeze with terror or apathetically wait for the worst. The English either get mad as hell or annoyed. The other day I was caught on the outskirts of a little place when they came over. There was a woman with a dog close by. She had her shopping bag with her. She asked me to hold the dog.

"I can't understand Jackie," she said apologetically. "He trembles so when the bombs fall. And he tries to run away."

The bombs fell. There was no shelter so we stood there. Finally she said with great annoyance, "I had so much marketing to do today. Now I shall never get it done."

They went away and the little old lady and her dog went on into the village to do the marketing.

Gossip is very important in our lives here. There is no theater; the moving picture houses all close at seven. There is no night life as we knew it two months ago or as New York knows it today. Anecdotes about Winston Churchill continue to be our pet diversion. I met Christiansen in Fleet Street today and he told me a lovely story about Winston. (We all refer to him as Winston just as Washington correspondents refer to Roosevelt as F.D.R.)

In the cloakroom of the House yesterday a Member of Parliament buttonholed Churchill. "Winston," he said, "it is time we struck back. Every night they come over killing women and children. All our bombers do is to attack military objectives. It would be a great pleasure to a lot of us if you would order the R.A.F. really to lay Berlin low."

Churchill nodded sympathetically. "I know how you feel," he said. "It would indeed be gratifying to know that the people of Berlin had to live as our people live. It would be nice to stop bombing only military targets to give the people of Germany who follow the leadership of that inhuman monster a taste of what we are getting. Yes, it would be a great pleasure but—" he added sadly, "business before pleasure."

The R.A.F. pilots react to the news that German bombers are overhead with the same sparkling enthusiasm and wide-eyed radiance which would animate a chorus girl who has been offered a second-hand bunch of orchids. The other day I was at an airdrome. The boys had just come in after a really tough fight over the Channel. They did the same thing that we all do after a day's work at the office—they headed for the nearest bar. In this case it happened to be their own mess, right at the airdrome. Pink gin is the navy drink; scotch and soda is the army drink; beer is the R.A.F. drink. After all, these boys who are winning the war in the air only make fourteen dollars a week. So we drank beer together at the mess and had some laughs together and then the mess steward, a dignified old gent who looked like a fugitive from a haunted house, came in to announce dolefully: "Gentlemen, hos-tile aircraft in vicinity." The kids who had been out over the Channel all morning laughed.

"Give us another round, William," the squadron leader yelled happily.

The old steward looked very unhappy. He went out and got another round of beer.

"Beer, beer. Always it's beer, and hos-tile aircraft in the vicinity. The Commanding Officer told me to report it." He kept grumbling as he served the beer.

"It's a wonder we're not all murdered in our beds," I told him.

"These young gentlemen, beggin' their pardon, wouldn't care if we were," William said, looking at the pilots reproachfully. "An' the place full of hos-tile aircraft."

We heard the familiar sound of the German bombers. You could tell they were very high. The pilots lounged around drinking their beer. If they were needed a phone would ring and they'd be in their Spitfires in two minutes. They knew that twelve of their pals were outside, alongside their airplanes. Why weren't they called? The Jerries overhead were reconnaissance planes perhaps. Anyhow, every Commanding Officer within a hundred miles knew they were here. Maybe they were running into an antiaircraft barrage ten miles back. The command knew what it was doing. Meanwhile there was beer.

Finally William came back. "The air alarm is finished, gentlemen. The hos-tile aircraft have gone. I have been asked by the Commanding Officer to tell you."

"William, you take care of the beer, we'll take care of the hos-tile aircraft," the squadron leader said.

One might expect such a reaction from fighting men but when you get it from civilians it somehow startles you. I was at a movie the other night and I might add that it was *Rebecca*. The film had only been running about fifteen minutes and the sinister Mrs. Danvers had just made her appearance when the sirens sounded. The picture stopped abruptly and the stage was lighted. The house manager walked to the center of the stage and said: "Enemy aircraft are in the vicinity. Those who wish to leave may get return tickets at the door. There is an air raid shelter in the cellar but this is a good strong building and I really think you'll be as well off where you are."

The man next to me got up hurriedly. He was with his wife and boy. He said to his wife with resignation, "After all I'm an air warden. I suppose I'd better go. I'll be back soon, honey."

She said: "How annoying. Just when the film was getting exciting. But, dear, I'll remember and tell you everything that happens."

That night I heard the German radio expert report that London had been panicked by the German bombers. I got a cable from New York saying: "Reports here that London in flames." There was damage in London all right; there will be further damage, but I don't think that London will be ruined or that London will be panicked. They never panicked Jack Dempsey, did they? Sure, they hit him and hurt him and London will be hit and hurt. In fact it is being hit and hurt today. But what of it? These people know they are in a war and know they've got to take a beating before they've won it. They know that lots of them are going to be killed. Every time the bombers come over they shake the debris out of their eyes, go to the nearest pub, have half a pint of bitter and say: " 'Ow many did we get today?"

You never get used to bombing. I never met a man yet who has. During the past six months I've been under plenty of German bombers who were dropping those Hitler Croquettes and I never got my hair mussed. But I get scared every time. So does everybody else.

I started getting scared at Montmédy when that was the front. Then it seemed as if everywhere I went was the front and always it was being bombed. I was scared at Tours and at Bordeaux and coming across the Channel and I've been scared in London a hundred times. I've been scared in a dozen Channel villages. It seems as if I attract bombers.

I only mention all this to explain that when I tell of the way London has reacted to the bombing we have nightly I'm not talking academically. I am an expert in the business of being scared. It isn't the career I might have picked for myself but there it is. Sure, people in London get scared—if they didn't they'd be half-wits. But once the bombing is over they don't carry a hangover. The French did. But here in London once the noise of the thing is out of your ears you shake your head and it's "business as usual." I'm talking about people I know. I'm not talking about heroes. I never met a hero outside of Hollywood anyhow. I'm talking about the man in the subway. Here he's the man in the pub or the girl on her way home from work or the Fleet Street reporter or the waiter who brings you your tea in the morning.

As a matter of fact the West End crowd (that corresponds to a New York, Monte Carlo, Colony, Stork Club, "21" crowd) reacts the same way. The other night we had an air raid just after dinner. I was at the Savoy Hotel. The dining room was crowded. Everyone was happy, contented, and this feeling was reflected in the playing of the band. The band was just playing along, not going to town really. The band was playing the song "Franklin D. Roosevelt Jones." The harsh shrill note of the siren cut through

the music and for a moment everyone who was danc-
ing faltered and hesitated. Bombs fell close enough to
rattle the glasses. Then the band really went to work.
When it came to the last line " 'Cause he's Franklin
D. Roosevelt Jones" everyone in the place was singing
it, shouting it, yelling it. You couldn't hear the sirens
or the guns or the bombs now. No one went downstairs to the air raid shelter. The band repeated the
song and the staid brigadier generals; Guards officers
in their plaids and their wives with them; Navy captains loaded with their four stripes of gold braid—
everyone laughed and sang the song and everyone
shouted the last line " 'Cause he's Franklin D. Roosevelt Jones."

There's still magic in that name to a lot of us.

A bit fed up with London, I drove to Kent to spend
the week end with a man and his wife. It was lovely
and charming there and life was going on quite
normally. On Monday morning when the husband
and I were leaving the wife had a request to make.

"Listen, darling," she said to her husband, "when
you come down next week end please bring me some
gunpowder."

"Whatever for?" he asked.

"Well," she said in a matter-of-fact tone, "our
bridge club in the village meets every Tuesday but
now we make those Molotov Cocktails—you know,—
the ones we will blow up the tanks with. I have plenty
of bottles and I have tar and petrol but I have no
gunpowder. I don't see why you can't get me some

gunpowder. Sarah's husband gets her all she needs. And last week old Lady Ethel brought enough for thirty cocktails."

"All right, darling," he kissed her good-bye. "I'll bring some gunpowder if I have to steal it."

CHAPTER ELEVEN

I WISHED THE KID LUCK!...

AT EACH END OF THE AIRDROME there was a large
tent. This was one of the airdromes nearest to the
Channel and there was a squadron of Spitfires here
at this end and a squadron of Hurricanes at the other
end. A squadron consists of twelve planes, and the
twelve pilots were sitting in the tent listening to a
portable radio.

It was just six in the morning and it was the kind
of morning when you feel good to be alive.

Each squadron had a crew of twenty-four to look
after it. The crew was playing football, the kind of
football we call soccer. They had taken two chairs
from the tent and that made one goal. They needed
something for the other goal, and one of them suggested using two Spitfires. It was probably the first
time in history that Spitfires were used as goal posts.

The squadron leader had plenty of ribbons on his
breast. He had downed eighteen German planes. But
he was quite young, of course. He took me aside and
said: "I want you to meet the new kid who joined us

yesterday. A nice kid. See if you can spot his accent. He hasn't been up with us yet. Today will be his first show."

He called the pilot over and introduced me to him. I spotted his accent all right. We hadn't spoken a dozen words when the telephone in the tent rang. It rang once, twice, three times. That meant get ready to take off. It had a loud ring and the ground crew stopped kicking the ball around. The squadron leader answered the phone. He listened for a moment and then said: "Twelve or more heading for convoy off Dover. Yes, sir." I looked at my watch. It was exactly 6:05.

The squadron leader said gaily to the pilots: "A scramble." And all of them ran to their planes. The R.A.F. has a language all its own. A scramble is a fight. All he said to his men was, "A scramble."

Each pilot climbed into his Spitfire and put his helmet on. They didn't look like kids any more now. The helmet covers everything but the eyes and the nose. In the helmet are earphones and there is a white aluminum disc that hits your mouth and you talk into that. When you are up in a Spitfire you can talk to any member of your squadron. Mostly, of course, you listen. You listen to your leader, who is the boss of the show.

The squadron leader, whose first name was Cecil (we are not allowed to give the full names of the men in the service), took off. The others followed him. As the last plane got off the ground I looked at my watch. It was 6:09. They fly in sections of three.

The first flight led by the squadron leader is called
the Red Flight. The second is called the Yellow
Flight. The third, the Blue Flight. The fourth, the
Green Flight. If the squadron leader in front wants
to give a quick order he just calls into his white
aluminum disc: "Yellow Section sharp right-hand
vertical climb."

The Spitfires circled once to gain height and then
went up to 10,000 feet. This wasted perhaps four
minutes but it was important. The twelve German
planes might turn out to be more, perhaps thirty
Messerschmitts and Heinkels, and, in a scramble,
altitude can be an excellent weapon working in your
favor. Then the Spitfires headed for the convoy.

Down at the other end of the airdrome the Hurricanes started to roar. Twelve of them rose and went
on to join in the fight. Ours was only one of a dozen
airdromes in the vicinity. I could imagine the same
thing happening at each one of them. The Hurricanes were now circling. After a while you get so you
can tell one plane from another. In the air the Spitfire looks like a thin, straight needle. The Hurricane
is humpbacked. They shot off in the wake of the
Spitfires.

The time passed very slowly. They would certainly
be back within an hour and a half because the fighters
carry gas for only that length of time. It was just
seven when the Spitfires appeared. I watched them
and there was something uneven about the formation.
Then I realized that one of them was missing. They
landed and taxied up to the tent.

It is routine that when a squadron returns, the squadron leader gives a report to an intelligence officer of what has happened. Then each pilot reports. In that way a pretty good idea of the damage done to the enemy can be obtained.

The squadron leader said: "We met them about halfway over the Channel at 14,000 feet. There were about twenty Heinkels and at least twenty-one 109's and 110's. We came out of the sun and got fairly close. I sent a four-second burst at a Heinkel. It dove toward the sea, smoke pouring out from it. A 110 got on my tail, and I banked away and into a cloud. I angeled up another thousand, keeping my flight together. Ran into two Heinkels. At 100 yards I sent a three-second burst at one of them. He went to pieces and crashed into the sea. I followed the other Heinkel, which had turned. He dove and I followed, sending two bursts. He was badly hurt and I followed him all the way down. At 500 feet he burst into flames. I followed and saw him dive into the sea. I collected the squadron. There were no enemy aircraft in sight. We came home."

"Is that all?" the intelligence officer asked.

"Yes," the squadron leader nodded. "Except that Isaacs failed to return. He got separated from the squadron. I don't know how."

"I saw him." The pilot who spoke was a lad named Douglas—he was very tall and very slim and he had a baby face. "I saw him with two 110's on his tail. By the time I got to him they had got him. He went down. Had no chance to bail out."

One by one they told their stories. When they had finished, the intelligence officer studied notes he had made. "I make it seven confirmed enemy casualties and four unconfirmed," he said.

The pilot must actually see a plane crash into the sea or to the ground before it can be listed officially. He must pledge his word of honor that he has seen it. When you see a story saying that twenty German planes were downed the chances are that another eight or nine suffered the same fate.

The squadron leader said to me: "You didn't get a chance to talk to the new kid, did you? He put up a great show today."

The new kid was looking at his Spitfire. There was a hole in the fuselage you could stick your fist through.

"You put up a great show," the squadron leader said to him. "When did you get hit?"

"Just when I was on the tail of an Me. 110," he said ruefully. "I felt a little jar and then all my controls went haywire. I sent one burst at the Me. but didn't get him. Even my sights were acting funny. But it was fun while it lasted."

The kid turned to me and grinned.

"Seven weeks ago today I was in Laredo, Texas. I've been dreaming about doing this since the war started. I went to Ontario, enlisted and within three days was on a boat."

"They looked at his log book and found he had 1,800 hours," the squadron leader said. "That's why they hustled him over so quickly. He only needed a week's training to get accustomed to the way a Spitfire handles."

"It's a beautiful airplane," the pilot said. "I never saw anything handle quite so sweet."

The boy's name is Art Donahue and because he is an American I hope the censor will relax his rule about the use of names. Laredo, Texas, might like to know what Art Donahue is doing. Right now there are about thirty Americans in the R.A.F.

A single Spitfire landed and taxied up to the tent. A pilot climbed out, came up and saluted the squadron leader.

"I was told to report to you, sir," he said.

"Righto; meet the boys and have some tea," the squadron leader said.

There was an awkward silence for a moment. Everyone was thinking of Isaacs but no one said anything about it. Now the squadron was a squadron again.

Outside, the mechanics were working on Donahue's Spitfire. They worked incredibly quickly. It would be ready in an hour, they said.

Young Douglas said rather shyly, "Would you like me to show you how a Spitfire works?"

He was like a child wanting to show off a new toy. We walked over to his Spitfire and he told me to climb in. I did. Douglas began to explain things and his face was lighted with animation.

I sat there and handled the controls. The glass in the windshield is nearly three inches thick and it is bulletproof. At the top of the windshield there was a mirror for all the world like the mirror in your automobile.

"That's a big help," Douglas grinned. "Maybe you notice that none of us wear collars or ties. We spend half our time turning our necks to see what's in back of us and after a scramble we usually have stiff necks. The mirror tells us if an airplane is directly on our tail."

"What do you do then?"

"Pray," Douglas laughed. "Pray and get the hell away from him."

The stick on a Spitfire is a very small wheel about five inches across. There is a small button on the wheel. When you are flying you hold the wheel in your right hand. You hold the throttle with your left hand. When you sight an enemy airplane you try to get your back to the sun. Then you go after him. You keep peering through the sight. The sight appears to be nothing but a heavy, oblong piece of glass. But once you focus on it you see a red circle in the glass and two lines that cross. When the enemy plane is within the circle and when it is covered by the two crossed lines you merely press the button with your thumb.

"Don't do it, though," Douglas said quickly, as he saw my hand go for the wheel. "The safety catch isn't on."

When you press the button eight guns bark. The guns are in the wings. Because they are flush with the wings you don't see the guns. Douglas said he liked to shoot at 200 yards. There are twenty-four

little clocklike instruments on the dashboard of a
Spitfire. Douglas explained them one by one. He
really knew what they meant. He even explained a
whole gadget which is strictly a "hush hush" instru-
ment. Anything new and secret is labeled "Hush
hush." In the R.A.F. the boys have orders to destroy
secret gadgets in case of a forced landing in enemy
territory. All I can say about this one is that it is a
link with headquarters. "This wireless is pretty wonderful," Douglas said. "We can talk to one another
and listen to one another. This morning for instance
we didn't sight the Jerries until we were about ten
miles over the Channel. Then the squadron leader
saw them and he yelled to us, 'Tallyho! Tallyho!
there they are.'"

He laughed.

"We all got more or less separated when the
scramble began. I was after a Heinkel when one of
the lads called to me: 'You'd better look behind you;
better look behind.' I did and saw a Me. coming at
me. I did a sharp vertical climb and got away. Then
I saw the lad who'd warned me and damned if there
weren't two of them on his tail. I yelled back, 'So
had you; so had you.'"

"Did he look behind?" I asked.

"That was Isaacs," he said simply.

I started to get out of the cockpit. It is quite a job
to get out of a Spitfire. I asked Douglas how it was
possible to bail out.

"I found a swell trick to bail out," he laughed. "I
was in real trouble three days ago. Luckily I was way

up, but my ship was on fire. I couldn't get out of the darn thing. So I unfastened my belt, turned the airplane over on its back and just fell out. That Channel water is damned cold, too, let me tell you."

"Who picked you up?"

"One of those little motor torpedo boats. They can certainly step. They go about forty-five miles an hour. You know the squadron leader? He's a grand chap with a great sense of humor. He had the nerve to tell me I bailed out just to get a new uniform."

"That's doing it the hard way," I suggested.

We went back into the tent. It was almost ten. At ten this squadron would be through. Then they'd fly inland a few miles and have an eight-hour rest.

But at fifteen minutes to ten the phone rang once, twice, three times. The squadron leader said, "Yes, yes; that's all right; we don't mind. Twelve off Folkestone. Righto."

The motors roared into action. The pilots ran to the planes. I gave Douglas a boost onto the wing and then he climbed into the cockpit.

"Good luck, kid," I shouted.

"I might need it," he yelled back, grinning.

I guess he needed more luck than I had to give him. Fifteen minutes later the boy was dead.

CHAPTER TWELVE

IT'S STILL CHURCHILL'S CHANNEL . . .

AIR MARSHAL HERMANN GOERING, July 31, 1940:
"And the German air force dominates the North Sea
and the English Channel."

"Here comes Jerry," a cheerful voice called out
and then we knew that we were in for it. I was standing aft by the gun turret. There were two good guns
there. Two men, one named North and one named
Simpson, crouched behind the guns, grinning with
pleasure. They had once been fishermen. Well, actually, this trawler we were on had once been a fish-
erman, too. But now it had been converted into an
armed trawler and it was nursing a convoy through
the Channel.

There were twenty-seven of us in all, and one destroyer. We had just entered the Straits and we were
off Margate. It was North who had called out, "Here
comes Jerry."

No orders came from our captain. He was standing on the bridge, smoking his pipe. He didn't have

to give orders. Every man knew what to do. It was a beautiful afternoon. The sky was blue and friendly-looking and the few clouds that hung against it hardly moved.

We could see the French coast quite clearly to the left. We could see the English coast, of course, to the right, and I knew that just a mile or so back of the coast there were airdromes and that now pilots were hurrying into their Spitfires. The whole machinery used to protect this convoy was swinging into motion.

We steamed on, making six knots only, for the slowest ship always sets the pace. Then we heard the German airplanes. They were very high, and at first we couldn't see them. Then the helping sun hurled its rays against the German planes, and the rays flashed and shimmered as they hit the smooth body surfaces. So we were able to locate them. When airplanes fly low they are dark and black. When they fly high they are silver and almost transparent. There were six of them and they were at least 20,000 feet high. They were directly overhead, which is where I like to see German bombers. When they are directly overhead they can't hit you.

When a plane going three hundred miles an hour drops a bomb, instead of falling straight down, the bomb travels in the direction of the plane for some little distance. When a plane directly overhead at sufficient height releases a bomb, the bomb will fall about half a mile away from you. So you always like to see the airplanes directly overhead. The danger is past then for the moment.

North was cursing softly. These planes were too high. But the shore batteries opened up now. The blue sky was suddenly miraculously studded with small puffs of cotton. But they were far below the Germans. Then our destroyer fired a few shots and, strangely, they left black puffs in the sky. They were using a different kind of explosive. Then we heard the loveliest sound in the world—the high, singing note of the Rolls-Royce motors of the Spitfires. The Germans wheeled sharply toward France.

The Spitfires appeared, twelve of them, buzzing angrily because their prey had escaped. They circled twice and then turned for home, their motors wailing dejectedly. Serenely, we steamed on, twenty-seven little ships.

My trawler led the convoy. I went to the bridge and stood by the captain. He had given me the run of the ship. "I've got just three things to ask," he had said when I came aboard. "Always wear your tin hat; always wear your Mae West and then," he added, grinning, "when the sun is over the yardarm always report to the messroom."

I didn't know what the last one meant at first. I soon learned. At eleven that morning I was on deck. The first officer grabbed my arm.

"The sun is over the yardarm," he said. "Come on below, can't keep the captain waiting." We went below. The captain and four of his officers were there.

His fifth officer was on the bridge. The captain poured the gin. It's gin and water or gin and bitters for His Majesty's Royal Navy at eleven o'clock every morning. It is a mild gin and although there are no restrictions no one has more than two or three. The officers in His Majesty's Navy are taught to handle drinks as they are taught to chart a course or to tie knots. They are not the hardest group of drinkers in the world but they are certainly the best. This eleven o'clock ritual replaces afternoon tea in the navy. Tea is still sacred to the R.A.F. and to the army, but when the sun is over the yardarm it's gin and water for the navy.

"The worst experience I ever had was years ago in the submarine 167." The captain had been with submarines most of his life. "It was pretty awful. The bloody cook thought he'd give us some cabbage. The smell of that cabbage cooking was the worst thing I've ever smelled. It took days to get the smell out of the ship. After that it became a regulation never to cook cabbage in a sub."   . .

A sailor came into the messroom. "Enemy aircraft approaching," he said.

Unhurriedly the captain rose and we left the room. I went to the bridge again. The Channel is full of mine fields. The captain grinned and pointed to a buoy. It's name was Hope. A good omen, that.

We were opposite Ramsgate now, about ten miles of the Channel behind us. In the distance we could see the immaculate white cliffs of Dover rising steeply, cleanly from the sea. German planes were off

Dover. We heard them and then we saw them. They were a bit lower this time, fifteen of them.

"Come on, Jerry," the captain said, thinking aloud. "We're ready for you."

I looked back once. Our convoy was strung out in a straight line, twenty-seven of us. Then the Dover guns began to fire. We heard them faintly. As the airplanes came closer, other guns on the shore picked them up. The white puffs were quite close to them. Then once more the Spitfires came. Their motors were singing joyously this time. The Germans didn't turn tail. If anyone tells you that the German pilots are cowards tell him he's nuts. They aren't nearly as well trained as the English pilots but they are brave. Silver streaks flashed across the sky, Spitfires diving and then zooming upward. The bombers tried to keep their formation, leaving the fighting to their escort of Messerschmitts.

Our guns swung into action. There were two on the bridge, each a double gun. They barked angrily. Our heavier guns aft were in action too, their slim noses pointing skyward. Our destroyer was firing and then most of the firing stopped. The Spitfires had closed in, and the sky was a jumble of German and English planes, whirling and writhing. They were bits of silver mercury crisscrossing the blue of the sky. The bombers were half a mile away now. This was the danger point. They dropped their bombs. They were being hurried and harried by the persistent Spitfires. The bombs fell short. One fell a hundred yards away, throwing up a huge cascade of water.

The bombers had had enough. They turned towards France. Spitfires and Messerschmitts flashed in and out of the clouds, playing a game of hide-and-seek, with death the referee. Then a burst of black smoke came out of the tail of a Heinkel bomber. The airplane dove, leaving an ugly black trail behind it. It dove slowly, or it may be that it just seemed slowly. A thousand feet above the water it recovered and straightened out. It limped toward France and then suddenly it came apart. It wasn't a live, pulsing thing any more; it was a shattered piece of junk and it dropped like a stone.

The Germans were in full flight now. They were almost over French territory. The Spitfires were finished. They turned for home. Through my glasses I watched the retreating German airplanes. One of them faltered, seeming to lift its nose high in the air, and dark smoke started coming from its motor. Two tiny specks dropped from the airplane and then something white billowed above each speck. The airplane dove gently into the Channel. The two men who had bailed out floated down slowly into the Channel but near the French shore. Through my glasses I saw a plane coming from the shore. It was flying very low. It was a flying boat sent out to pick the two pilots up. It landed and presumably rescued them. Then it took off and returned home.

We steamed steadily on, still twenty-seven of us. It was dusk now and we were opposite Hell's Corner.

That's where you turn just before you reach Dover. Here and there masts stuck up, reminders that this wasn't a parlor game we were playing. In the early stages of the war the magnetic mines did a lot of damage. Now all ships have a gadget that immunizes them against magnetic mines. I looked around with my glasses.

It was dusk now and the dying sun was painting the waters of the Channel with a magic brush. Here the water would be a deep purple, here a burnished copper, here a flaming gold. Every sunset you see is the finest sunset you've ever seen. No two are alike.

Even the London papers call it Hell's Corner. It is the most dangerous ten-mile stretch in the world. Once upon a time the boats of fishermen dotted the water and girls like Gertrude Ederle swam through the water from Cap Gris-Nez to Dover. But now it is Hell's Corner. Looking across to the French coast, you could see both Boulogne and Calais. That's where the big twelve-inch guns were. That's where they had been a few days ago.

They had shelled a convoy here off Hell's Corner a week before. I had watched the shelling from the high vantage point of Shakespeare Cliff. From there I saw the huge orange bursts of flame shoot upward and heard the dull boom a second later and then, thirty seconds after that, saw the shells land, throwing up tremendous cascades of water.

We steamed into the water off Hell's Corner and waited. Were German gunners now plotting the course of those twelve-inch shells? We were only making two knots now because the tide was soggy and heavy against us. We should be an easy target and yet those guns were twenty-two miles away. The dusk deepened a little and Dover, flanked by its white cliffs, brightly green at the top, looked like a toy village with its red gabled roofs and its two tall white church steeples. We waited.

I walked aft to the rear-gun turret and climbed into it with North and Simpson, who had once been fishermen. We were all a little nervous. Actual danger never scares you much; the anticipation of danger does. We waited.

"This is a lucky ship," North said. "We have a lucky captain and I'm a very lucky bloke myself. Got a little lucky piece here. Look at it."

He showed me a small silver medal with the picture of a saint upon it.

"That's lucky," he said complacently. "I found it years ago. That medal brings you luck at sea."

There was an inscription in French on the medal. I read it. "Do you understand French?" I asked North. He said that he didn't. I handed him back the medal. What was the use of telling him that this was a medal dedicated to St. Bernard and that the French inscription said that St. Bernard was the patron saint of skiing? The good saint probably felt a bit out of place in a gun turret on a trawler crawling through the Channel.

We steamed on, and it was very quiet. It seemed as though the world had stopped breathing until we got safely through. No orange glare burst over the French coast. I walked back to the bridge.

"For three nights the R.A.F. lads have been over there trying to find those big guns," the captain said. "They've been dropping a lot of bombs. It might be that they've destroyed the guns." There was a rather hurt note in his voice. Other convoys had been shelled, why not his?

We steamed on and gradually we all relaxed. That was it, the R.A.F. bombers had silenced the big guns. The sun hesitated reluctantly and then plunged down behind the towering heights of Shakespeare Cliff. Darkness, our ally, had come to help us.

We steamed on steadily, twenty-seven of us. The little trawlers and the little merchant ships raised their black smoke impudently. A slight breeze had sprung up.

Far ahead, four foam-flecked white specks appeared. They grew larger and now we saw them to be four small, fast ships. They were to be with us during the night. From the stern of them flew the red-and-white flag of Poland. They are the fastest thing afloat carrying guns. At top speed they can hit well over forty knots. They carry depth charges and anti-aircraft guns. We expected to be attacked during the night by the German E boats—fast, 103-foot ships something like American Coast Guard Cutters except that they carry torpedoes. The little motor torpedo boats can throw a smoke screen around a convoy. The darkness grew, and the little Polish boats disappeared, but now and then we could hear their powerful Isotta-Fraschini motors. There was only a small chunk of moon showing but the night was studded with stars. A message came through to the captain from the wireless room. He handed it to me. "German aircraft shadowing bacon convoy." The captain laughed. "Bacon convoy indeed. That's the code word today for us. Why bacon? Well, the fishermen often use bacon for bait hereabouts. That's what we are, bait. I hope they'll try to swallow us."

Far above we heard the drone of planes, and then the English coast blazed with light. We were opposite Dover. A hundred white shafts of light pierced the darkness. From the bridge it looked like a bouquet of searchlights. Now and then an airplane would fly into the beam and then a dozen other beams would move like lightning, trying to hold it. Then the anti-aircraft guns would belch. These raiders were probably on their way to London. There were lots of them crossing now. It was just nine o'clock. I hoped they'd hit London at nine-twenty. We had a nightly pool in London as to what time they'd come over. I had drawn nine-twenty this week, a good hour. The whole coast was ablaze with the prying fingers of light, but the Germans were flying very high.

Now we heard more planes over us. The noise moved toward the French coast. These were British bombers en route to somewhere in Germany. Searchlights appeared from Boulogne and from Calais. We couldn't hear the German guns but we could see the red-and-purple tracer bullets knifing upward, cutting across the dead white of the searchlight beams. Then a British plane dropped a flare, and for a moment a mound of golden light flared. Then as it began to die, a fierce, angry burst of flame shot into the air. A bomb had landed, then another and still another. This would be about where those big guns were located. The still night air carried the double-barreled sound of the bombs exploding. A big bomb makes a throaty "wumph-wumph" sound.

We sailed along, showing no lights, hugging the friendly darkness of the Channel water, hugging the English waters of the Channel. We sailed along, still twenty-seven of us.

For an hour the searchlights on both shores kept poking inquisitive fingers into the night. Then gradually they died out and we had the Channel to ourselves. A man wearing earphones stood on the bridge. He was in charge of the anti-submarine detection instruments. His instruments showed that submarines were near. We would know exactly where the submarines were and we'd hustle over there and drop our depth bombs. We were out of the Straits now, and dawn found us out of sight of land. This was submarine territory. The men leaned over their guns, scanning the skies and the sea. No one had slept; you don't sleep on trawlers.

It was golden dawn and the sun bathed the little ships, gleaming brightly on their gray sides. We steamed on steadily, hitting seven knots now, for the tide was helping us. No boats appeared. No submarine came. The hours passed quietly and the crew looked disappointed. They'd had little opportunity to do their stuff. Then in the distance we saw land. It grew and it grew, and the captain smiled. "Pompey," he said.

No naval man ever calls Portsmouth by its real name. Portsmouth has always been, is now and always will be, "Pompey" with the accent on the first syllable. This was our port. The beaches of Portsmouth gleamed whitely. We steamed into the harbor.

Our little trawler led the way proudly. The others followed. They seemed a little self-conscious but quite pleased with themselves. Twenty-seven of us had started. Twenty-seven of us had arrived safely.

The captain said, "Sorry we couldn't give you more excitement. But it was a pleasant trip, wasn't it? The Channel behaved pretty well. And now, m'lad, you'll notice that the sun is over the yardarm."

We went into the messroom. We poured our gin and water. "God bless you," the captain said. It was his stock toast. Then he said, "What do you think of our little Channel?"

I raised my glass. "I think enough of it to drink to it. Here's to Churchill's Channel."

Air Marshal Hermann Goering, July 31, 1940: "And the German air force dominates the North Sea and the English Channel."

CHAPTER THIRTEEN

ALL AIRCRAFT RETURNED SAFELY ...

THE BIG WHITLEY, one of England's largest bombing planes, looked harmless enough. She dozed there
in the sun, her grotesque camouflage making her
look like some weird but not particularly vicious
prehistoric animal. Old Brownie and I walked under
the belly of the bomber. In another three hours Old
Brownie was going to climb into the airplane, fly far
into Germany and then drop 3,600 pounds of bombs.
Old Brownie had very fair hair, very large, gentle,
blue eyes and a wisp of a blond moustache, and he
wore a slightly apologetic air. He was one of the
veterans of this group. That's why they called him
Old Brownie. Actually Brownie was just twenty-
three.

It was shady and cool under the big monster. The
ground crew had just finished "bombing up" the
planes. The bombs were lying in two parallel rows.
Some were 500-pound bombs, others were 250. They
were freshly painted a bright yellow and they looked
innocent enough. Brownie explained to me how they

would be released. They could be dropped in "sticks" of six or individually. Brownie slapped one of the 500-pound bombs on its fat rump. "Want to send a message to any friends in Germany?" he asked.

I took out a soft pencil and wrote on the bright yellow side of the 500-pound bomb, "with love and kisses" and then under that I signed my name.

"That'll bring you luck, Brownie," I said, and Brownie laughed. We climbed up into the plane and Brownie showed me where he sat. It was a cozy little nest. Ahead of and below the pilot's cubbyhole was another little cubicle. The man who dropped the bombs made this his home. He would lie there on a sliding wooden panel and from there he could look ahead and below. He had a gun there and his bomb sights and a row of buttons to release the bombs. Sometimes he would release them and sometimes the pilot would.

Back of Brownie was a chair for his co-pilot and a small desk where he did his navigation. This bombing group flew only at night, and on dark nights proper navigation was pretty important. Behind the co-pilot there was a space for the wireless operator. Then we walked back through the long plane fuselage. There were flares and flare chutes and other paraphernalia of the bomber trade neatly arranged there.

In the very rear was the gun turret. This made the Whitley one of the best of all bombers. The Whitley had a real sting in its tail: four guns that shot 4,000 rounds a minute. The turret revolved so that you could sight a Messerschmitt above you or on either side of you.

We climbed down from the step and Brownie looked at his watch. It was time for getting final instructions. We walked past the other nine planes that were to take part in tonight's raid and went into a building on which there was a sign, "Operations."

Upstairs there was a large room with about sixty chairs and desks in it. There was a blackboard on the front wall and a large desk on a raised platform. It looked like any other schoolroom. It was called the "Briefing" room. Behind the desk, looking at maps, were two men: the squadron leader in charge of tonight's raid and the intelligence officer.

The pilots and wireless operators and gunners and observers looked a bit astonished when we walked in. It was the first time a civilian had ever been permitted in the "Briefing" room.

The wing commander stood up and said, "Here are your instructions for tonight. You all have target maps in front of you. The primary target is an airplane factory at (we can't mention the names of targets or give the full names of pilots). We don't know much about the defenses around the primary target. When you get there, use your own judgment. You'll see by your maps that it is about seven hundred miles from here. The weather should be good all the way. If you can't find the primary target or if the visibility is bad when you reach it, your second primary target will be ——. You know all about that."

There was a stirring in the room and faint smiles

appeared on the faces of the boys. I knew about that secondary target too. It was in the Ruhr, which is full of oil tanks and munition factories. In the army they talk of a place that is to be stormed as an "objective" but in the R.A.F. it is always the "target."

"You know what to expect there," the wing commander continued. "Now you should be over your primary target at midnight, or a few minutes afterward. If you find the target, drop your bombs and give us a signal that you are okay and are returning. If you go to the secondary target be careful not to bomb northeast of it. That is a residential section. Be very careful to avoid that. Incidentally, you will carry pennies with you. Drop them if possible over residential sections."

"Pennies" today was the code word for pamphlets. Millions of pamphlets were being dropped over Germany every night.

Now the intelligence officer said a few words. He told what he knew of both targets and what defenses the boys would be up against. This seemed to bore the fifty silent lads in uniforms. There were just fifty of them, five to each of the ten bombers.

"Incidentally, on the way back," the intelligence officer said, "watch out for small lights near any of the Channel ports. If you aren't being teased too much when you are over them have a look and see what they are. Any questions?"

"What is the moon tonight and how much light will we have?" a pilot asked.

"Quarter moon," the intelligence officer said. "Day-

light will come at about 4.30 A.M. You must leave
your target by one to be clear of enemy territory before daylight."

There were no more questions and, like youngsters
in any classroom, the boys piled out of the door. It
was teatime now. We went to the officers' quarters
and tables were piled with bread, butter, cakes and
large pots of tea. Brownie and the tall Scotsman
named Pete and chunky little Red and I sat and
talked and I was the only one thinking of the peril-
ous night ahead. After tea the men went to study
maps in the chartroom.

Two hours of this and it was dinner-time. The
whole group assembled in the clubroom for cocktails. They sat around smoking, laughing, having
sherry, beer, whiskey or Martinis and it was all very
pleasant. The O.C. (officer commanding) entered
and everyone stiffened for a moment and then, when
he smiled, everyone relaxed. The R.A.F. officers are
all too busy to bother with useless formalities. They
are very close to their men. It was a pleasant dinner.
These boys seemed completely indifferent to what
faced them soon. Either that or completely confident.
Then they drifted away to change clothes.

The ten planes were being warmed up. It was
almost eight but the sun sets very late in England
in the summer. I walked with Brownie to his plane.

"Wish you were coming along," Old Brownie said
cheerfully. "Looks like a nice night."

The setting sun was just casually putting an end
to a beautiful day. The clouds were very high and

there was practically no breeze. All twenty motors (the Whitley is two-motored) were humming now. I walked with tall Pete to his airplane. Pete looks like Gary Cooper, lanky, amiable, slow-talking.

"Wish I had a book to take along," he said.

In my pocket I had a paper-bound detective story called *The Green Diamond Mystery*. I gave it to him, but wondered when he'd get time to read it.

"I'll let the kid fly for the first few hours," he said.

"Have a good trip," I told him, "write to me every day."

He grinned and climbed up the tiny ladder into the huge plane. They were all giving the motors a final blast at full throttle. Then the huge, dozing earth-bound planes suddenly became live, mobile things. They didn't look lazy and unwieldy now as they trundled around into the wind. After fifty feet their tails lifted and after 200 yards their wheels raised. One by one, they lifted themselves into the air, at two-minute intervals. In the air they looked slim and full of eager vitality. They circled once and then surely, swiftly they soared away and soon even the sound of their motors died.

The airdrome seemed strangely quiet now and lonely as a college campus looks and feels in vacation-time. Some of us played cards for a while and then several pilots who weren't working tonight took me to the local pub in a near-by town. We talked of many things, sitting around there, but we didn't talk about the ten pilots and their crews who were now gradually approaching enemy territory. I couldn't think of anything else. I could imagine Pete reading his detective story, stopping every few minutes for a quick check with his crew. I could imagine Old Brownie and Alec sitting there casually, lightly fingering the controls, looking at a dozen instruments at once.

Time passed very slowly. We went back to the airdrome. Everything was pitch-black. The dying moon, having only one quarter of its life left, was giving little light to a blacked-out world. It was bright enough inside of "Operations." Then I went into the holy of holies, the Operations room. This was the heart of the airdrome. Here were the wireless and the telephones and maps, and now and then the wing commander would make marks on the maps.

The clock moved slowly. Once the yellow signal was given, meaning that an unidentified aircraft was in the neighborhood. Other reports came in. On a map we followed its course, wondering whether it was an enemy bomber. Then the word came that it was an English training plane. England is so full of defending fighting planes that it has become hazardous to train bombers at night. They are no sooner in the air than they find a Spitfire or a Hurricane nosing inquisitively against them. There is always the danger that the bomber might be mistaken for a Heinkel or a Dornier. Now most of the training is done either in Canada or over France.

It was a little after midnight and now reports began to come in. The pilots of our bombers had reached the target; had found it; had dropped their bombs; had started home. Pete checked in with his one word "Okay." So did Alec and so did Red. There was a chart on the table and, as word came from the radio room, the squadron commander would check them off, one by one. By one o'clock nine of them had checked in and were now on their way home.

But we hadn't heard from Brownie yet. No one mentioned it. We listened to a German radio maintained for the amusement of German pilots. It was good music. At ten-minute intervals, over and through this music, would come three staccato dashes, repeated three times. This was a German beacon. The music was just to keep the pilots awake. The Germans use beacons a lot and the R.A.F. know where each is located and sometimes use them too.

Officers who had left orders to be called at two o'clock drifted into the room. They looked at the chart. Everyone was all right but Brownie. Still no one mentioned it. I had only met Brownie twenty-four hours before but now I felt sick with worry. Someone brought in tea. We drank it and talked about a speech Churchill had made the day before.

I was visualizing long fingers of white light reaching up for Brownie, covering him with light. I imagined him trying to swerve away from it and meeting another long finger coming through the sky. I saw him desperately trying to get into the merciful blanket of a cloud and I saw the tracer bullets go up after him and pom-pom guns, and then the heavy stuff battering the sides of his plane.

It was four o'clock now. I walked out onto the field. A faint dawn was showing in the east but above it was cloudless. A wind from the west brought a chill with it. Then faintly I heard the sound of a motor. It became a roar and then the plane came into view. It was flying low and its lights showed brightly through the thinning night. Green lights, the "Come on in" signal, blinked from the field and the big ship landed. It taxied to its hangar. Figures climbed down and I walked to meet them. Tall, lanky, Pete the Scotsman had landed safely.

"You can have this book back," he said. "I guessed who did it in the first ten pages."

"How was the trip? Any trouble?"

"No, they threw some stuff at us but it wasn't bad. Damn cold though at sixteen thousand feet—fifteen below."

Another plane was approaching and then another. While one landed, another circled. Two more approached. The chickens were coming home to roost. But what of Brownie? One by one they landed. The crews walked straight to the Operations room to report everything that had happened. I went back and listened.

Pete said, "We found the target at 12:05. There were cumulus clouds at four thousand that were breaking. I dropped the one 'stick' and then went back and dropped the rest. The clouds thickened and

I turned for home. Listen—about those lights over the Channel. I had a good look at them. That's phosphorescence, I think. It's shallow in there and it may be that the light from the moon hits the rocks on the bottom and that light is reflected."

Alec reported, "Found the target. The clouds were getting thick. Dropped two sticks but couldn't see result."

Red reported, "Never could find the target. Too many clouds. Went to the secondary target. They got a lot of new light stuff there and plenty of searchlights. I dropped a couple of flares. I guess they figured it was me going down in flames and the searchlights all went out. It was easy to pick out the target then. I dropped my bombs and saw a big explosion. Hit it, I guess."

Questions were asked. I listened, keeping one eye on the door. Then it opened and a fair-haired lad with large blue eyes and slightly apologetic look walked in. It was Brownie.

"You scared us," I told him. "We never got your report."

He looked blank. "I forgot all about the damn thing," he said. "Now I'll catch it."

The wing commander looked up, saw Brownie and then wrote, "All aircraft returned safely." Brownie gave his report casually as the others had. Then we all went to the mess for bacon and eggs and hot tea. Nine crews were there joking, kidding one another.

England is a country that produces a great many old fools who somehow find their way to high places.

England doesn't produce many young fools. These kids weren't fools. They'd done a great job tonight and they knew it but they weren't going to get serious about it.

"Say, I got a scare just before reaching the target," Alec said to Red. "A big aircraft came out of a cloud not two hundred yards away. I told the boys to watch it. I was hoping it was a Heinkel. It looked like one. And who was it? It was Red."

"Yeah, I saw you, too," Red said, munching some bacon.

"Where's Eddie?" someone asked.

"He'll be right along," someone else said.

"Bet he'll have a swell story," Brownie laughed. "He'll say, 'There I was, at twenty thousand feet, hanging by my knees to the rudder bar. There I was right up there in the sky with a feel of ice on my wings and twenty Messerschmitts around me. I got them, one by one, and then went down and dropped my bombs on a Dornier factory. The flames shot a thousand feet in the air.'"

Eddie walked in then, a big, tousled-haired kid who was twenty, two months ago. He looked very unhappy.

"I could not find the main target," he said dejectedly.

"Did you bring your bombs back?" Red asked.

"No," Eddie said casually, "I dropped them on the secondary target. I looked around and found five big oil tanks. I dropped my bombs on them and say, you should have seen those flames! They were——"

"They were two thousand feet high," Brownie said.

Eddie looked hurt and ordered bacon and eggs. Brownie and I walked outside. It was six-thirty now and a brilliant dawn was touching the ugly hangars, making them almost beautiful.

Brownie yawned, "How about some shut-eye? This has been a long day for you."

"Sure," I said sarcastically, "a long, tough day. How far did you fly tonight?"

"About 1,500 miles," Brownie said.

"That's more than halfway from here to New York," I said.

"That's a flight I wouldn't want to make," Brownie said. "All over water? Not me. This was a cinch compared to that. I'll see you later. How about Pete and you and me going into town tomorrow? We'll have the night off."

I said, "Sure, that'll be swell," and then I went to bed.

CHAPTER FOURTEEN

LONDON—CITY OF CAVES . . .

THE BANSHEE WAS WAILING and it sounded eerie in the dusk. It trailed away but the echo of it hung in the air which was heavy with the weight of the darkness. There were nearly a thousand of us standing there. We were in front of the Camden Town subway station. An iron gate had been stretched across the entrance. Two policemen guarded it. "There's no room below," they repeated again and again. "Not room for another person."

Camden Town is the workers' section of London. The Camden Town subway station was eighty feet below the street. Since late afternoon families had been going into the subway. They had thermos bottles filled with hot tea; they had paper bags of food; they had toys to quiet the children. Those who arrived first were now sleeping below safe, because there was eighty feet of earth and concrete between them and the street surface.

Then faintly we heard the drone of German planes. The air barrage began. Some of the guns were close and you tried to shake the noise of them out of your head. Whenever there was a lull you could hear the so-familiar hum of bombers above. Nearly a thousand of us huddled there in the darkness. A bomb fell. We heard the fiendish whistle of it as it dropped from a plane perhaps 20,000 feet above us. Its high-pitched scream grew more piercing and then it landed. It fell a block away. The concussion of it made us sway as one person. The policeman opened the gates. "Better to be in here and crowded than be out there getting hurt," he said gruffly. It was only professional gruffness; his eyes were dark with worry.

Men, women, children filed in quietly, patiently. There was no fear on a single face. A few babies who had been awakened by the noise began to whimper a little. We climbed downstairs to the subway platform. The concrete stairs were crowded. You had to step over people. The platform was packed with people lying on the concrete. Some were playing cards.

This is how thousands of families live at night in London—far under the ground. Usually the working man of the family arrives home about five-thirty. He'll find some hot mutton in the stove being kept warm—if the gas main in his section hasn't been destroyed. He'll find tea on the stove too. But his wife and children have long since left for the safety of the subways. It is first come first served and they went early. When Pop finishes his meal he joins them. They've saved a place for him. It may be cold down there and the air sticky with the feel of hundreds of people packed closely together—but it's safe. He and his family accept their lot philosophically. This is a new world and they adapt themselves to it.

A man with an accordion came in and was greeted with friendly banter. He played "Tomorrow is a Lovely Day," "There'll Always be an England," and even the kids joined in the singing. Then he played the most popular song of the day, "The Nightingale Sang in Berkeley Square." Several "incidents" had occurred in Berkeley Square during the past month and the accordion player commemorated them by singing his version of the song calling it "A screaming bomb fell in Berkeley Square." They all laughed at that. All but me. I lived in Berkeley Square.

It was getting late now. The subway dwellers impose a nine o'clock curfew on themselves. The accordion player pillowed his head on the accordion. A heavy quiet settled over the reclining forms.

The guns and the bombs seemed far away. A train pulled in. Those who were asleep never woke, for noise is so much part of our existence in London these nights that it is only quiet which disturbs us because it seems unnatural. Londoners are quick to adapt themselves to a new environment. Today more than half of London sleeps underground in public shelters, in subways, in cellars. Every office building has its own shelter and thousands of workers remain in them all night.

I got on a subway train. I stopped at each station and always it was the same. These people were adapting themselves to a new way of life. Many of the women wore heavy slacks. Stores now advertise "shelter slacks" or "siren suits." I went out as far as Hampstead. Hampstead is a section where fairly well off people live in fine detached houses. But tonight these families were sleeping on the concrete of the subway platforms and stairs. It was difficult to get off the train. Before I could step on the platform a woman had to move her sleeping child. I picked my way over a thousand sleeping forms before getting to the stairs. I chatted with one family.

"You get used to it," the woman said. "Of course the air is bad, but at least we know that we're safe. I wish Millie would hurry home, though."

Wherever she and her family slept was "home" to her. Millie, a slim, bright-eyed girl finally came. With her was a young man in army uniform.

"This is my fiancé," she introduced him. "It's his first day of leave." "Never thought I'd spend my leave in the underground," he laughed.

The night wore on. It grew cold and sometimes people stirred uneasily. Some still read newspapers in the dim light. Those who had tea shared it with those who didn't. Two policemen were on watch. They kept walking up and down through the crowd. Their chief concern was to see that restless children didn't roll off the platform on to the tracks below.

"What time do you turn them out?" I asked.

"Turn them out? I'd like to see anyone try to turn them out. They usually leave when the 'all clear' sounds."

All year the Government has been building brick shelters. The streets and sidewalks are lined with them. They are about seven feet high. The people don't like them. They prefer to live underground. In these brick shelters you can hear the bombs screaming, you hear them exploding, you hear the constant roar of the guns. Since the nightly blitz began we have learned one thing—if you don't hear them they don't exist. In even a shallow underground shelter which probably wouldn't help at all if a bomb fell close, the sound is deadened and you feel a sense of security.

The brick shelters are deserted these nights. The Government in the beginning disapproved strongly of using the subways as shelters. The people and the police calmly ignored the Government's attitude. Herbert Morrison was made Minister of Home Security. Morrison grows in stature each day. He gets things done. There was a new subway line under construction. On his first day in office Morrison opened it to the public.

I came out of the stagnant atmosphere of the subway for a breath of fresh air. The streets of course were deserted. It is virtually impossible to get a cab at night in London and subways stop at ten o'clock. If you go out at night you walk. I walked a few blocks. It was very dark. The guns were firing at a terrific rate. Apparently most of the roofs in this section were slate roofs because when the spent shrapnel fell on them there was a sharp crack as though someone were firing a rifle. There was too much stuff going up and then coming down so I ducked into a pub.

"The shelter's down that way," a barman said. "Everyone's down there."

The basement had been converted into a shelter. At one end perhaps twenty people slept soundly. I went to the other end where a bar had been improvised. Three men were playing darts.

"Good shelter this," I said. "At least you can't hear the blasted Jerry," one of the men said cheerily. "My old woman and the kids have been asleep down the other end for two hours. We sleep here every night."

We had a glass of beer and I teamed with one of the men against the other two and we won. They had to pay for the beer.

"Getting like moles we are," one of them laughed. "Living underground like bloody moles. But it ain't bad."

I went out in the night again. It was much quieter. London is a ghost town at night. You never meet anyone on the street. Now and then the fire engines or ambulances would roar by. You never see them because they carry only the smallest sidelights. The street intersections bother you at night. You never know when you've reached the curb. Then you constantly bump into lamp posts or mail boxes. Walking around London at night hardly comes under the head of good clean fun.

I reached the more familiar region of Fleet Street. I went into the *Daily Express* building. The last edition had been put to bed and sixty feet below the

ground the huge presses were rolling. Reporters,
desk men, rewrite men, sat about, some dozing, some
playing cards. They'd stay here until daylight or
until the "all clear" sounded. Like everyone else they
too lived many hours each day underground.

Upstairs Christiansen, wearing a tin hat, sat at his
desk looking over the last edition which had just
come from the presses. He pointed at the headline
—"London has quiet night."

"They only set two fires all night," he explained
when I asked what had been quiet about the night.
Just then a big bomb fell not too far away. The
windows rattled but didn't break.

"That's a fine headline," I told him. "Oh, sure,
a great headline. A quiet night, hey?"

He just looked hurt. I walked on down Fleet Street
and into the Strand. I stopped at the Savoy Hotel to
see how people slept there at night. The Savoy has
an elaborate shelter. There is a doctor on duty twenty-
four hours a day. Several members of the hotel staff
took nursing courses and they stand by. They have
built a miniature hospital complete even to a small
operating table. It was quiet here. People who live
in the West End hotels have it a bit easier than those
who sleep in the subway shelters. The cots are comfortable; there is a canteen open all night and there
is always a drink within reach. The East End has
to get through an air raid on pale ale. The West
End can afford whiskey.

You meet the strangest people in the shelters. I
walked to Claridge's. I walked through their shelter

—huge, roomy, well-heated. I met a reporter whom I knew and we chatted for a while.

"Not so loud," he whispered. "You'll wake the Queen." He jerked his thumb towards the corner. "What Queen?" I asked. "Queen Wilhelmina," he said. "She sleeps over there. And Prince Bernhardt has the cot next to mine."

I walked to another expensive West End hotel. This too had a magnificent underground shelter and more than two hundred people were sleeping there. Here was the lovely Lady Diana Cooper and there, shedding his ministerial cares, was Duff Cooper himself. Some of England's wealthiest and most influential people slept here. Beyond the actual shelter was what had been in peace-time the women's Turkish bath. Now alas, it was tenanted only by males, the most prominent of whom was Lord Halifax. But they were all comfortable and the air conditioning was good and there was tea and whiskey and sandwiches should anyone awake. There were nurses to take care of and quiet the children. It was very pleasant.

From there to the Piccadilly Circus subway station was only a step. Piccadilly Circus is the Times Square of London; it is the largest subway station in the city. A policeman on duty said there were nearly three thousand people asleep down below. I walked down; there was no air conditioning here; no nurses; no hot canteen. The platform and the stairs were jammed with what in the dim light looked to be shapeless untidy bundles.

I walked home. It had been a long night but I had seen something the world hadn't seen for thousands of years. I had seen a city asleep in caves under the ground—modern caves to be sure, but caves none the less. It hadn't been a pleasant night.

I heated a can of chile con carne. I ate that and drank a bottle of beer and made believe that I was in Carrizozo, New Mexico.

CHAPTER FIFTEEN

BRITAIN'S LABOUR BOSS . . .

BILL ADAMS is a printer who makes about twenty-eight dollars a week. Bill lives in a small house in a suburb of London. On Sunday night Bill has the same supper that several million other Englishmen have. He has cold beef, tomatoes, boiled potatoes and hand-picked onions. Just as he was about to sit down to dinner last Sunday the telephone rang. A voice said, "This is the office of the Minister of Labour. Hold on."

Then in a moment there came a voice that Bill Adams knew well. It was a voice with a strong West-country accent, a voice belonging to the second most powerful man in England.

The voice said apologetically, "Bill, this is Ernie. Could I come around for a bit of supper?"

"Sure, Ernie, come along," Bill Adams said heartily. And then he went to the kitchen to tell the Missus to slice another tomato. Ernie likes tomatoes.

Within a few minutes his Majesty's Minister of Labour entered the house. He sat down wearily, for though it was Sunday he had put in fourteen hours of work that day.

Bill Adams said, "You look tired, Ernie. Tell me just one thing. Are you on top of the job, have you got it in hand?"

Ernie Bevin nodded thoughtfully. "I think so, Bill. I really think so. There is only one thing that bothers me, Bill, I seldom get a chance to see the boys. They keep me working pretty hard, Bill."

Bill Adams told the story in his local pub a couple of days later and I heard it there. He and Ernie Bevin are old friends. Bill said that Ernie hadn't changed a bit since he had become a Minister of the Crown. Good people don't change, Bill Adams said. People like Ernie Bevin and his pal Dan Williams and Herbert Morrison. No, good people don't change. And, mark you, Ernie Bevin is a good man, Bill Adams added to his friends in the local pub.

Today England is saying that Ernest Bevin is a good man. I think it is very likely that tomorrow England may say that Ernest Bevin is a great man. Not all of England likes Bevin. The muddlers don't like him because he cuts right through the lovely red tape that they and their ancestors have taken so many years to wind about the machinery of governmental operation. The old-school-tie boys don't like Ernie Bevin because his rugged, devastating honesty and his admitted keen intelligence mock everything that they and their class deem sacred. Bevin stopped going to school when he was eleven, but today he is the smartest practical economist in England. The Communists, of course, don't like him because he kicked them out of his trade union years ago. But the man in the street loves Ernie Bevin.

The man in the street likes Bevin because he thinks that Bevin is going to make this a people's war, a war fought by the people and for the benefit of the people, not a war fought by one class for the benefit of one class.

The outsider, as he calls himself, is no respecter of school ties or tradition. The man in the street listens with intense excitement to the magnificent speeches of Winston Churchill and the man in the street wants to believe in the Prime Minister. But, asks the man in the street, is Churchill going to realize that this war belongs to the Ernie Bevins of England, not to the old gang to whom Churchill so far has been true?

Why, asks the man in the street, did 71-year-old Neville Chamberlain hold a position in the Government until a month before his death? The man made every conceivable blunder possible for a diplomat to make. Instead of giving his country guns he gave England widows. Lord Halifax, the dignified and dreary Foreign Secretary, is still in the Cabinet. Never once did he raise his voice to dissuade his former chief from perpetrating the gigantic mistakes of the past. Sir Kingsley Wood, the little man who wasn't there, is still governing the Exchequer. Sir Kingsley, who during the peaceful days of autumn, 1939, made soporific speeches lulling the nation into sleepy quiescence and into the belief that airplane production was in every way satisfactory, is still a powerful minister. And dismal Sir Samuel Hoare, who is called Soapy Sam in Fleet Street, is the inept advocate of England's cause in Spain.

There is so much that is progressive and magnificent about Mr. Churchill's Cabinet that the man in the street hates to see it held back by the legacies of failure whom Churchill still tolerates. The man in the street is proud of dynamic Herbert Morrison, Minister of Supply, and of Lord Beaverbrook, who is making up for past sins so vigorously. It was he who contributed to the inertia and complacency of the nation by crying loudly, "There will be no war." But when it came he rolled up his sleeves, and now his great personal courage, his tenacity and his mental capacities are devoted heartily to the nation's welfare. The man in the street admires the idealism and enthusiasm of Anthony Eden, Secretary of State for War. And then there is Bevin. Bevin, of them all, speaks with the voice of the man in the street. Bevin is their advocate. He too wants to make this a people's war.

Ernest Bevin was born in the Somersetshire village of Winsford fifty-nine years ago. He quit school at the age of eleven to work on a farm. His first salary was sixpence (ten cents) a week. Work on the farm gave him a magnificent physique but little else. He was still in his teens when he went to Bristol to drive a streetcar. Then he switched to driving a truck. At twenty his salary was ten shillings a week (two dollars) plus commissions, an average of three dollars more. His joy was to sell mineral water and soft drinks to the Bristol pubs. The pub in England is the poor man's club to a far greater extent than it is in America. The man in the street goes to his pub every night for a glass or two of beer and a game of darts, and he goes to air his political views and to hear the views of his neighbor. Pub people liked young Ernie Bevin and they liked the vigorous way he expressed himself on political questions. There was a vacancy on the city council and Dan Williams and other pals persuaded him to stand for the office. His opponent was a huge longshoreman. One night Bevin was driving his truck, delivering his cases of mineral water to a water-front pub. He heard his opponent making a speech on a dock and he drove his horse-drawn wagon closer.

"Who is Bevin?" the longshoreman sneered. "An outsider from the country. He is no good, he is a . . ."

Bevin listened. He had never before heard invective directed against himself. A slow rage filled his big frame. He got down from the wagon. He forced his way through the crowd. Without a word he reached for the big longshoreman. Then he hit him. When the man got up Bevin knocked him down again. Then Bevin picked him up and threw him into the river. Bevin looked around to see if any wished to take up the man's cause. There was no one who did. Luckily there was a scow tied to the dock and the men on it managed to drag the miserable longshoreman out of the water before he drowned. Luckily, because had he drowned Bevin would not now be Minister of Labour.

That method of direct approach, of solving problems the direct way, has always characterized Bevin. He hates red tape and silly regulations, he hates insincerity and pompousness. As a matter of fact he hates politics.

His fight with the longshoreman had a rather unhappy sequence. Running on the Labour Party ticket, which in 1908 was considered a radical, crackpot movement, he was beaten. He was beaten, but his fine showing thoroughly scared the gang in power. They decided to get rid of him. They passed the word around to the Bristol pubs that Ernest Bevin should be blacklisted. For weeks he could not sell one bottle of mineral water. He went to his boss and tried to quit his job.

"I'm not making any money for you," he said. "You've been paying me ten bob a week for nothing."

"I'll be the judge of that," his boss growled. "Don't let them lick you, Ernie. Keep at it."

Bevin has always had the knack of attracting people to him. It wasn't long before he became interested in labor unions, always called trade unions in England. He became a minor official in the dockers' union and soon attracted the attention of Ben Tillett, who was to English labor what Sam Gompers was to American labor. It wasn't long before he became Tillett's right-hand man, his "trouble shooter."

But it wasn't until 1920 that the name of Bevin meant anything. Then he made a speech. The transport workers' union was miserably paid and worked miserable hours. A court of inquiry to discuss their pleas was held and Bevin made an eleven-hour speech on the men's claims for more pay and better working conditions. The case he put was masterly and unanswerable. The men won every point and the name of Bevin went all around England. The man in the street finally had a real advocate. Since then Bevin has devoted his life to the cause of labor. Eventually he became the leader of the transport and general workers' union, the largest union in the world.

A dozen times during the past decades he crossed swords with Winston Churchill. He opposed some of Churchill's policies when the latter was in the War Office. Again when Churchill was Chancellor of the Exchequer Bevin fought against him. Honors were about even and both men came out of these skirmishes with mutual respect and admiration. But it was still a shock to the old gang when Churchill made Bevin Minister of Labour in his cabinet. Bevin didn't know the rules, they wailed. He was . . . he was just an outsider.

Bevin is big, burly, and he has the thick neck of a bull. And yet when you sit in his office at Montagu House, the ex-ducal mansion that is now the Ministry of Labour, his voice is curiously soft and occasionally his eyes twinkle behind his heavy horn-rimmed glasses. He is too busy to grant interviews. He'll let you sit in his office and he'll chat with you and discuss the problems that face him, but it is all "off the record." He thinks that this is no time for speeches or interviews. There is too much work to be done.

Bevin has a terrific capacity for work. He seldom

leaves the Ministry before midnight. Recently his wife wailed disconsolately, "If Ernie sleeps until after 5.30 in the morning he thinks he has wasted half his day."

A few months ago Bevin was given powers never before held by any man in any democratic government. He was given complete power over the jobs held by civilian workers in England. It is up to him and him alone to decide what industries are essential and what ones are superfluous. Actually Bevin could go to Waterloo station tonight, enter a train and say to the first man he met: "What is your job, what are you doing?"

The man might say, "I am a tea taster," or "I am an interior decorator."

Bevin could say, "That isn't helping to win the war. Report tomorrow at Hyde Park with a pick and shovel. We need you to dig trenches."

He could go into a fashionable West End bar, find out what every man there did for a living and then immediately send them to more useful jobs. He can decide on working hours for every man in England and it is he who settles their wages. There is no appeal. And yet to date there has not been one complaint. Bevin has shifted thousands of workers from less useful jobs into munition factories and other essential industries. He has told employers that there can be no cutting of wages. And employers have such confidence in his fairness that not one has written a letter to *The Times*.

I might add that I learn about England by spending my time at a Royal Air Force mess, spending my time on the beach at Dover with the army men, spending my time with local defense volunteers in places like Sevenoaks in Kent or a dozen places like it, spending my time in the pubs of rural England. In these places you hear England talking. Twice a week I go to the House of Commons but that is like going to the United States Senate. For the most part you hear politicians talk in these sacrosanct halls. But you don't hear England talk. I hear England talk every day.

I know the men Bevin has worked with all his life. I can't quote Bevin because he has made an ironclad rule that he won't be quoted. But I spend evenings with his best friends. I play darts with them and have my pint of beer with them. I hear them talk about Bevin.

"There will be no defeatism in our Cabinet while Ernie is there," one of them chuckles. "You know Ernie is the only man in England who can call a general strike. I know if Ernie said the word nine millions of us would quit working tomorrow. That's a weapon Ernie has over the lads in the Cabinet. There will be no Pétain in our Cabinet. If one crops up Ernie will say, 'Well, gents, the general strike starts tomorrow. How do you like that?' Well, they wouldn't like that, so there won't be any of that French stuff in our Cabinet."

That's what Ernie Bevin's friends say, about 9,000,000 of them. They know that Ernie will never use this terrific power he has unless he feels that it is for England's benefit. He will probably never use it, but the weak sisters in the Cabinet are afraid of this power. They respect Ernie Bevin even when they don't like him. Only a half-wit would not respect Ernie Bevin. And it is comforting to know if you are interested in the English cause, as I am for one, that he is in Churchill's Cabinet. He is a very tough man, a very tough man indeed and very patriotic too. He happens to love this country called England.

You can live in the fashionable West End of London and never live in England. To know England you must go into the local pubs of London and Liverpool and Manchester. You must drop into the country pubs of Kent and Surrey and play darts and have your pint of bitter and keep your ears open. There you hear the voice of England. There you hear praise of Churchill, the leader, but always there is the undercurrent of wholehearted admiration for Bevin.

Today Bevin is Minister of Labour. Tomorrow I am sure that he will be Vice-Premier and thus be in name what he is in fact, the second most important man in England. And the day after tomorrow? The voice of England whispers, "How can they keep Ernie down? Mark ye well, he'll be our next Prime Minister."

CHAPTER SIXTEEN

DIRECT HIT . . .

FIRST THERE'S EDDY DUCHIN. I mean for me. I'd rather hear Eddy Duchin play the piano than hear anyone else in the world play the piano. But Tim Clayton comes second. I live in a very large apartment house and Tim Clayton and his band play in the restaurant, which is below the street level. I usually have dinner there and listen to Tim Clayton and his band.

Tim looks like Paul Whiteman, which is no distinction, but Tim is just as grand a guy as Paul is, and that is a very definite distinction.

Tim has a relief band in the restaurant which gives him a chance to sit with me now and then and have a drink. Last night I had dinner alone and when I was through Tim sat down and had a drink and then he thought he'd go outside and have a look at things. He came back ten minutes later looking anxious.

"It's bad tonight." He shook his head. "Worst night we've had. Some of them are falling very near. And those heavy anti-aircraft guns are making a hell of a noise."

He looked around the crowded room. It was midnight. Half the men present were in uniform: officers on leave. Everyone was fairly gay; as gay as we can get in London these days.

"These chaps on leave, now," Tim said slowly. "Pity they can't have their few hours in peace. Down here you don't hear the bombs unless they're very close and you don't hear the guns. But they're getting closer. I tell you, suppose I play loud as hell? Even if they fall close they can't hear them then. I'll play 'Stormy Weather,'" Tim added.

"Not loud enough, Tim," I told him. "Play 'Begin the Beguine.' Give it lots of brass."

Tim slid onto the piano seat and his lads deftly replaced the members of the relief band. The music never stopped. Then Tim started "Begin the Beguine." Cole Porter, who wrote it, would have screamed with horror. Tim played it as though it were a Sousa march. Maybe it wasn't good but it was loud.

The dance floor was crowded now and men were laughing and girls were smiling with their eyes. Faintly, because we were below the street surface and because of the music, I heard the horrible "crump" sound of bombs falling. They weren't far away. But here in the night club none had a thought for bombs.

Tim played a popular song and the whole band

sang it—but loud. Tim played for an hour and his
relief band appeared.

It was just one o'clock. I walked through the air-
raid shelter to the elevator. It used to be the cellar,
and the walls are still whitewashed. There were
eighty people there asleep on mattresses. A heavy
door cut off the restaurant from the shelter. Faintly
you could hear the music. You could hear the anti-
aircraft fire much more clearly. It was almost con-
tinuous. The light was dim and I picked my way
carefully over sleeping forms. One very small, very
white-haired and very old lady was sitting up knitting. When I saw what she was knitting, I gave her a
startled look. She smiled and shook her head, "My
daughter is going to have a baby soon," she said.

"If it is a girl I hope she won't call it Siren," I
told her.

Hundreds of girls are going to curse the air raids
we are having now. Every time a girl is born during
an air raid proud parents name her Siren. I walked
through the shelter to the far end. There is a service
elevator there which goes through to the roof. It was
quite dark and then I heard a throaty growl. I looked
around and discovered it came from a brown cocker
spaniel.

I said, "Don't growl at me or I'll slug you." Then
the dog whined a little. I asked him if he wanted to
go out. He yelped happily. The woman who owned
him was asleep and she had the leash tied around her
wrist. I reached down and untied the leash from her

wrist. He kept making small, whimpering noises. I said, "Shut up, you dope. If she wakes up she'll think I am stealing you."

He shut up all right. The dog and I got into the elevator and went to the roof. During air raids you aren't supposed to be on the streets or on a roof. But I had a key made for the door leading to my roof and I go there when it's a good air raid because it is quite a show. And then I honestly think you're as safe on a roof as anywhere. If a bomb scores a direct hit and you're in a vault in the Bank of England a hundred feet below the ground you are going to be killed. No air raid shelter is proof against a direct hit by a big bomb. Bomb fragments kill people and sometimes anti-aircraft bullets dropping kill people. That is what air-raid shelters are for.

My apartment house is ten stories high. If a bomb fell in the street, bomb fragments could not reach the roof. I like my roof during an air raid; I get nervous cooped up in a shelter with a hundred other people. People get afraid in an air raid. We all get afraid. Only a half-wit wouldn't be afraid. When you are alone on a roof you aren't quite so afraid. When you are with a hundred other people who are afraid, their fear somehow emanates from them and the cumulative fear of them all is somehow communicated to you.

Up on the roof I never feel very much afraid because I make believe it's all a show put on for my benefit by Billy Rose. I make believe the searchlights are something that Grover Whalen thought up to

make London more attractive at night. I make believe that the obscene tearing roar of the bombs is a
Fourth of July celebration and my nieces and nephews
are firing off Roman candles and firecrackers. That's
how you keep sane in wartime. If you accepted the
reality of it you'd go mad.

The dog and I got to the roof. I said, "What's your
name, pal?" He cocked his head at me and smiled.
If you have ever owned a brown cocker you know
they can smile. I tried a dozen names but he didn't
respond; he just sat there smiling. Then I said, "Come
here, Sweetheart." And he bounded into my arms and
that was pretty nice.

We were alone on the roof. It is a very big roof
about a hundred yards square. Sweetheart wanted to
play. He charged a chimney, growled at it, worried
it and then came back to me. He wasn't a bit afraid.
That was rather amazing.

I was staying at a farm in Kent last week end.
Bombs fell near us. There were sixty cows in the
meadow. When they heard the noise of the bombs
exploding they stampeded. They ran as fast as they
could until they hit a fence and then they turned and
ran back. A bull doesn't get scared. A bull gets mad.
When he hears the bombs he lowers his head and
charges until he hits something. At this farm they
keep the bull in a stall all day. He cost a thousand
dollars and it would be silly to let him kill himself
charging into a tree. But cows get scared.

When the cows stampeded, my host swore softly
under his breath. "No milk tonight," he said. "When

they get scared their milk is no good. It turns acid."

Horses get scared, too. But dogs don't get very scared. My little brown cocker wasn't scared. Maybe he was but he wasn't showing it. So we watched the show and it was a good show—wired for sound.

We were high. There were searchlights on all four sides of us. I counted 132 and then gave it up. Their white fingers cut through the night, disturbing the night which was meant for sleep.

A parachute flare filled the night. It lit perhaps a thousand feet from the ground. I stood there and found that I was saying, "Go out. Go out."

It didn't go out. It lit up half the city. It drifted down slowly, seemingly getting brighter. Now I could see Parliament; I could see St. Paul's Cathedral; I could see the outlines of the Ministry of Information Building. I was sweating a little and even Sweetheart was quite expectant. Above was the incessant "whoom-whoom" of the German planes. They desynchronize their motors so that it seems as though they breathe. They go "whoom" and then they hesitate and then they go "whoom" again. If their two motors are perfectly synchronized, the searchlights and the guns which work "by ear" could find their exact location.

Sweetheart and I waited. Then it came. The first one was so loud that the noise of it made me sway a little. The second was only slightly less loud. The flare died out and now a small red glow appeared. Those bombs had found a target. The glow grew sullenly, reluctantly, but it kept growing and now it wasn't a glow any more. It was a fire.

The night was full of noise. They were dropping more bombs. Two other fires appeared. They were big fires. Sweetheart and I stood on the roof watching the fires—watching a part of a civilization being destroyed. I looked at my watch. It was 2:30. Then I realized I could tell the time because the fires had lighted the sky. I looked over the city. Six million people were down there—practically none of them asleep. I imagined white-faced women in air-raid shelters; I imagined tight-lipped men beside them clenching their fists, swearing softly and impotently. There is no defense against death from the night.

I stayed an hour. There were three big fires. Sweetheart was asleep. A spent machine-gun bullet or a bit of shrapnel hit the roof. Then another hit. I thought it was time to retire. Sweetheart didn't want to leave.

"Death is for suckers," I told Sweetheart. "Let's get out of here."

I took him down below and told the elevator man to tie him up to his owner. I went to my apartment. I have two beds there and Arthur Christiansen was asleep in one and Bill Stoneman was asleep in the other. That was all right. Neither of them had slept for two days. But Ed Beattie and Bob Low were helping themselves to drinks.

"I might as well live in the Pennsylvania Station," I said bitterly.

"You've run out of ice," Beattie said complacently.

"There's no soda," Low said. "What kind of hospitality is that?"

We sat down and argued about this and that. We

talked about the chances of getting hit by a bomb and we all agreed that if it had your name on it you can't duck it and if it hasn't your name on it you're all right. We all feel that way.

Then it came. The noise of it filled the room and hung there. We looked at one another in surprise. Our building had actually been hit. It seemed incredible. I opened the door. The corridor was hazy with smoke. Everything was very quiet now. We decided to go into the street to watch. "Let's not wake them," I suggested. "We'll tell them about it in the morning."

They thought that was a swell idea. We laughed at the thought of England's most brilliant editor and one of America's greatest reporters sleeping through a bombing. We went into the street. Lansdowne House where I live is very big. The bomb had fallen on the roof of an extension. The place was burning merrily. The bomb had fallen perhaps four minutes ago but already the auxiliary fire fighters were on hand. Except for the blaze there was no other light and there was no confusion.

"Evacuate the building," their chief said curtly and half a dozen guard men ran inside. That made us mad. It would spoil our joke on Chris and Bill. Then Beattie said, "You know I never thought of it but it might have been dangerous, leaving them there."

I looked at him in amazement. Then I realized what fools we had been. We get so in the habit of thinking objectively of being mere spectators that we can't accept the fact that in a siege like we are undergoing now we, too, might get hurt. We were a little ashamed of ourselves. Chris and Stoneman came out with bathrobes over their pajamas.

"We didn't want to disturb you fellows," I told them lamely. "We knew you needed your sleep."

They just glared. I said that Chris was the most brilliant editor in England. He proved it now. When he was awakened by the home-guard men pounding on his door the room was full of smoke. But Chris is a practical man. Automatically he put on my bathrobe, grabbed a bottle of my whiskey, woke up Stoneman and hurried to the street. He held the bottle out to us and we felt ashamed of ourselves. We hadn't thought of the whiskey. Maybe that's why we are just reporters and Chris is an editor.

The regular fire department had arrived. They worked quietly and quickly. Within thirty seconds four streams of water were playing on the fire. It was four o'clock now. Ladders were against the building and firemen were carrying hose. People from the apartment house came out in pajamas and bathrobes, some half-dressed, some carrying sleeping children, some carrying dogs. They stood there on the sidewalks watching the firemen work. Home-guards were all over, keeping people back so that they couldn't interfere with the workers. Home-guard men went from group to group.

"There is a hotel half a block from here," they said. "There is a shelter there, and mattresses for everybody. Please go there."

The strangely clad army obeyed. The blaze was

well under control. The bomb had fallen half an hour ago. In that time a large apartment house had been evacuated, shelters had been found for everyone and what might have been a dangerous fire was practically extinguished. England's civilian army had won another victory.

It was chilly now, and we were thankful to Chris for his thoughtfulness. Stoneman and Beattie went to their offices. This was too good a story not to file right away. There are no cabs in London at night during an air raid. They had to walk.

The dawn came to London now. She was a welcome visitor. It had been a long night. Some fools say that London is an ugly city. They have never seen London at dawn. It was a bright, cheery dawn that did everything but sing. German bombers don't bother us at dawn. London had had a beating during the night but in the dawn we saw no scars.

The firemen rolled up their hose. The home-guard men said cheerfully to one another, "How about a spot of tea?"

The fire was out. Two apartments had been smashed. A dozen windows had been broken. No one had been hurt. We went back into the house. Everything was normal. The telephone girl was still there. The elevator was working. Everyone was smiling and content.

"If that's the best old Jerry can do, we got nothing to worry about," the elevator man said.

The wail of the sirens cut through the dawn. This was the official "all clear" signal. In a few hours we'd hear the German radio. We'd hear, "London was bombed last night by the German air force. More than twenty terrific fires were caused by bombs exploding. Several important military objectives were destroyed. There were several thousand casualties and there was a terrific panic among the people. Half of London is in ruins."

My apartment is near the roof. I pulled away the black curtains we use to keep any light from showing. I can see half the city from my window. Not a single spiral of smoke was rising anywhere. Chris phoned the *Express* to find out what damage had been done. We learned that there had been five hundred bombers over the city. The damage? They had scored a direct hit on a boys' school, and a great many children who slept there at night had been killed. They had hit a hospital and thirty women had been killed. They had destroyed a warehouse containing silk and another filled with tea. In all they had killed about five hundred civilians. But civilian lives don't count today. A civilization is at stake.

Now looking over the city at dawn, you could almost see London shake the debris out of her hair. You could see the gallant city looking not down at its scarred streets and its mangled dead but upward toward the sun. It was a new day. London would face it calmly.

The telephone rang. It was Clayton.

"The boys and I are having a little poker game downstairs," said Tim cheerfully. "How about joining us?"

"This is a fine time to play poker," I told him.

"Any time is a time to play poker," Tim said.

"You have talked me into it, sonny boy," I said. He was right, of course. We had all been gambling with our lives all night. It might be fun to gamble with cards.

CHAPTER SEVENTEEN

THE MAN WHO DIDN'T QUIT . . .

THE MAN WHO DIDN'T QUIT has a closely cropped moustache and he is tall and straight. When he speaks the words come out sharply and when he talks of the betrayal of his country the words are bits of rounded hail dropping on a tin roof. General Charles de Gaulle, today the mouthpiece and leader of all free Frenchmen, is a very tough citizen indeed.

"France lost the war," he says with the confidence of a man who knows war tactics backwards, "for very definite reasons. These were: First of all, our military system did not bother to develop any mechanized strength in the air and on the ground; second, the panic which gripped our civilian population at the advance of the German mechanized units; third, the tangible effect the fifth column had on the minds of many of our leaders, and fourth, lack of coördination between us and our Allies."

In those few sentences de Gaulle told why a great nation was strangled to death in a few weeks. Behind each of his reasons lies one fundamental fault common to all—the horrible inefficiency of the General Staff, which still thought of this war in terms of the last war. The General Staff was proud of its Maginot Line. Its complacency communicated itself to the civilian population and finally to the Army.

France looked upon the Maginot Line as Americans still mistakenly look upon the Atlantic Ocean. It was a bulwark against invasion. France thought only in terms of defense. France believed that the war would be a war of position as was the last, not a a war of movement, of quick, smashing forays by large armies of tanks and motorcycles.

Only de Gaulle saw the handwriting on the military wall. As late as last January he sent a long memorandum to General Gamelin, who was then trying to win the war on blueprints. De Gaulle condemned the policy of passive defense and foretold the disaster it brought about. He pleaded for more, bigger, faster and better-armored tanks; he got nothing but a rebuke for this impertinence.

"Germany can still be beaten, even now," de Gaulle says. "But we must make use of the same weapons which she has used so successfully. Germany won with six thousand tanks and five thousand planes. She must be beaten by twenty thousand tanks and twenty thousand planes."

By a strange paradox the military theories of de Gaulle helped to defeat the French Army. In 1934 he published a book on mechanized warfare. De Gaulle was an obscure captain then known only for his personal bravery during the last war, when he was wounded three times. The General Staff frowned on the advanced theories he pronounced in his book. The book itself, *Vers l'Armée Métier,* received scant attention except from a few of his colleagues who thought as he did.

But one German read it, the astute General Hauss Guderian, who was just beginning to organize the mechanized forces of the Reich. Guderian made it his bible and when he swept through northern France with his army of twelve tank divisions, he used the paralysing tactics advocated by de Gaulle.

De Gaulle himself, during May, held command of the French tank army but he had only one division. His tanks performed brilliantly at Abbeville but he was only staving off the inevitable. He himself rode and issued commands by radio from one of the tanks.

He didn't have the enormous sixty-ton tanks used by the Germany Army. So confident was Guderian of the success of these tanks that many of them were armored only in front. From the beginning the Germans fought an offensive war with the possibility of retreat ruled out.

Today de Gaulle is the only articulate voice the free Frenchman has. Each day hundreds of weary French who managed, by some miracle, to escape from the cataclysm that engulfed their country go to his dingy suite of offices in St. Stephen's House on Victoria Embankment, asking to join his forces, pleading for a chance to strike a blow that might by some miracle breathe life into the corpse that is France. Within two months de Gaulle may be a half-forgotten name but if the miracle should happen he will emerge as the greatest and most patriotic of the French generals, the one man who refused to be a stooge for the miserable set of leaders who figured in the betrayal at Bordeaux. If de Gaulle's past is to be believed it is difficult to think that his future will be sterile.

In the beginning his career followed the military pattern. He graduated from St. Cyr as a lieutenant. He fought in the last war under the then Colonel Henri Pétain. He was wounded twice but each time returned to his regiment. Then, during the Verdun battle, he was wounded badly and taken prisoner by a German patrol. He made five abortive efforts to escape and each time had to endure the penalties for such failure.

His military career after the war was active except for a stretch at teaching in the military college at St. Cyr. During recent years his radical military theories received support from only one man in a high place, Paul Reynaud. During the first week of June he was recalled from the front by Reynaud to join the cabinet as Under Secretary of State for War. Reynaud felt that his colleagues were weakening under the pressure of both German military and fifth column strength; he wanted one additional strong voice to overcome the babble of the incompetent and the senile who through no fault of his had been put into the cabinet which he headed.

De Gaulle's tenure as a member of the cabinet was short-lived. When Reynaud was deposed at Bordeaux and Pétain put in, de Gaulle knew that it was all over but for the division of spoils. He hurried to London where he sent out an appeal to colonial generals for help.

One inducement was offered to French officers who fell in line with the Bordeaux government. The Germans promised them that their pensions would be safe if they behaved well. They held the safety cf their families over their heads as another blackjack. Thousands of French officers made their choice. They picked what they thought would be financial security and continued health for their families. They threw in their lot with the Bordeaux group which, day by day, becomes more of a puppet government.

De Gaulle, with the reticence of a professional soldier, refuses to condemn or even comment upon the action of his fellow French officers. He condemns the politicians and the General Staff bitterly, but he has not reproached the men who fought so brilliantly with him at Abbeville and at Cambrai during the nightmare of May. De Gaulle would rather discuss the lessons this war has taught the military world today. No country can say that distance protects it from the mechanized forces of another nation. He says, "To date the war has taught us that we have a real military revolution. If I were an American I would take these lessons to heart. America must be ready at any time with the necessary weapons to meet a modern attack, with mechanized forces of air, land and sea. If I were an American I would take for my slogan, 'We should do our utmost to save liberty in this world by all means and at any cost.'"

De Gaulle stood erect and strong; his face showed nothing but confidence. He terminated our talk with a short nod and a strong handshake.

Outside, in the badly lighted hall, men and women were waiting to see him. There were two small anterooms. In one a bespectacled lieutenant took the names of the callers, in another a Cockney lad answered a telephone. The shabbiness of the uncarpeted room and the derelict furniture, dimly lighted by uncertain bulbs, seemed a poor setting for bright dreams. But General Charles de Gaulle, the man who didn't quit, may emerge from the shabbiness of this old office building to make the dreams of hundreds of thousands of free Frenchmen come true.

In London we have our fingers crossed when we think of de Gaulle. We were thoroughly sold on him until the horrible Dakar fiasco. Whether he was entirely responsible for that blunder hasn't as yet been established.

Most of his officers dine at the Coq d'Or, a restaurant on Stratton Street, off Berkeley Square. I was there a few nights before the Dakar expedition. I noticed a group of his officers dining high, wide and handsome. The popping of the champagne corks almost killed the noise of the guns in nearby Hyde Park. I asked my waiter what it was all about.

"The frogs is having a victory celebration," he said.

"What are they celebrating—the Marne?"

"No, they are going to attack some place called

Dakar," he said. "Next week, I think. So they're celebrating their victory now."

That was news. That was big news. It was no good
for me writing for a weekly magazine but it was a
good newspaper story. I phoned Christiansen at the
Express and told him.

"Sure," he said wearily, "it's a swell story. But it's
strictly 'hush hush.' Everyone in London seems to
know about it and I suppose Vichy knows about it
and Berlin knows about it and Dakar knows about it."

In any case no one was surprised at Dakar when de
Gaulle's men arrived. Dakar will go down as one of
the greatest military fiascos of our time.

Was de Gaulle responsible? I don't know. Perhaps
he will still emerge as another Foch or Kitchener.
But I'd hate to have a dime bet on it.

CHAPTER EIGHTEEN

A PLANE IS BORN . . .

THE BIG HANGAR DOORS opened and there, poised in the entrance, was the new fighter. Even its drab brown, dark red and yellow camouflage markings couldn't destroy the slim, proud beauty of the airplane. Sixty-three days ago she had been only a mass of white lines on a blueprint; now she is complete, alive, ready for her first test. On the blueprint she had the speed of a Spitfire; the maneuverability of a Hurricane and a longer range than either. She was just one of many experimental fighters England is building today.

The airplane was wheeled out onto the field. Tommy, the test pilot, talked briefly to the designer. The designer, who also ran the factory and was responsible for production, puffed on a cigarette and then threw it away, half-smoked. He was a little bit nervous, as any father is at the christening of a brand-new daughter.

But Tommy wasn't nervous. Tommy had a small matter of 15,000 hours in his log book. Tommy had been testing planes for ten years. This was routine to him. He hitched up the straps of his parachute and climbed into the cockpit. He switched on the motor and it sang sweetly and truly. Tommy looked over at us and grinned happily. He never seemed quite at home on the ground. Then he opened the throttle. The airplane minced daintily across the field. He headed it into the wind. Then he let it go. The airplane sped past us and then, young as she was, took the air confidently, joyously. She was "air borne" now.

Tommy took her around the airdrome in wide, sweeping circles. He gained altitude; he descended in long, shallow dives. He made stall turns, gliding turns and then he "angeled up," as the R.A.F. lads say, to twenty-one thousand feet. Now we'd see how sturdy this new lass was. The airplane was only a white speck in the blue now—white because the sun was shimmering on its wings. We knew what Tommy was doing now. He was kicking his rudder to the left and simultaneously pushing his stick to the right; then he was pulling back the throttle, cutting the motor. In short he was purposely putting the new fighter into a spin.

If the blueprints were right she would come out of the spin. Otherwise Tommy would have to jump and the airplane would wind up a smoking mess of metal and wood on the ground. We could see the airplane coming down. It was in a spin; the nose was down and the airplane swung around dizzily. Now the nose came up and she was in a flat spin. That's the nastiest of all spins to be in. Then the nose shot down sharply, the tail came up and the airplane was in a nice, controlled dive. Tommy pulled out of it. He circled around the airdrome once, wiggling his wings. Then he landed and taxied up to us. He climbed out grinning.

"It's a gentleman's airplane," he said. "At four hundred miles I could handle the stick with two fingers. It's a grand kite."

A new fighter has been tried and not found wanting. It is forbidden to give any details of airplanes which have not as yet been officially accepted by the air ministry. It is sufficient to say that this new fighter is as good as anything in the air today. English aircraft production never stands still. Today we think of the Spitfire and the Hurricane as the best fighters ever built. The records of the R.A.F. prove this to be true. Yet every designer in the business is constantly trying for something even better. In time the Germans will catch up with the Spitfire and the Hurricane. Then England must have something just a little better.

Word went through the huge aircraft factory of the fine first flight of the new girl. Word sped from the machine shop to the experimental laboratory to the slowly moving production line that the factory's new aircraft had done nobly.

"She'll make the old Spitfire look like a truck," one grizzled old worker chuckled as he bent over his lathe.

"When better kites are built, we'll build 'em," another grinned.

No one in the R.A.F. or in the aircraft production end of it ever calls it a plane. Either it's an aircraft or a kite.

This was just another aircraft factory. Aircraft factories are scattered all over England. One hears reports from Berlin (via New York) that many of them have been destroyed by German bombers. If a reporter who is as objective as it is possible to be these days may say a word, I have visited a dozen aircraft factories (picked at random not by any minister of information but by me) and to date have seen no serious damage at any of them.

Take this aircraft factory where we are now. It is one of the largest aircraft factories in the world. Every two hours a bright, shiny airplane is nosed off the end of the production line and out of the big hangar doors on to the airdrome. The factory was established many years before the war began. Its location was known to every German, French, English and American aeronautical magazine. It still is. Yet the surface of its closely cropped grass expanse and the even symmetry of its gleaming concrete runways is scarred by one wound—a ten-foot bomb crater so small that it wouldn't attract attention in Piccadilly Circus. Once you are inside the huge buildings you can tell that you aren't in a Detroit factory—you can tell it because if you ask a workman for a cigarette he'll hand you a Player or a Woodbine. Otherwise it is much the same.

Outside there are anti-aircraft guns—plenty of them. On the roof there are spotters with their eyes glued to binoculars. The ordinary air-raid warning telling that German aircraft are in the vicinity doesn't interrupt work. If the aircraft gets near enough to be seen by the spotters they call "local cover" into microphones they have on the roof. That means "get under your benches" or "dive into the local shelters." On the concrete floor of the factory shelters have been built. They are about six feet high and three feet thick—heavily sand-bagged. The workmen have given names to these shelters and have put small British flags on them. One is called "The Duck and Fall In" and a placard embellished by a crude drawing of a duck with a bomb heading for it adds emphasis to the good qualities of that particular shelter. Another merely says "The Rush Inn, Caviar a Specialty."

But they aren't used much by the 6,000 employees of the firm. These men and women are too busy making airplanes to bother about bombs. Not long ago a group of R.A.F. fighter pilots visited the factory. They were entranced by the quick, efficient work of the men and women. They asked hundreds of questions. Finally a foreman patted their squadron leader on the back and said, "Listen, sonny—we are very busy. You and your lads go inside and have a nice cup of tea. We've got a war to win. All you lads have to do is fly 'em. We've got to make 'em and make 'em quick."

The glamor boys nodded silently and walked away. They knew that their job was fairly easy compared to the job that these 6,000 men and women were doing. The backbone of England's defense today is aircraft manufacture. I have been at a fighter command on a bad day. Eight fighters were lost that afternoon. The commander in chief picked up a phone. "Eight aircraft destroyed today," he said tersely. "When can you replace them? . . . Within an hour? . . . Fine!"

Within an hour eight Spitfires settled gracefully on the airdrome. Today no bomber or fighter C.-in-C. has asked for replacements in vain. Production is not only amazing but distribution is equally well organized. Lord Beaverbrook is a quick, small man. His airplanes are likewise quick and small. They spend very little time loafing in distribution centers. And they don't take long to build.

A day spent in an aircraft factory tells you why. The 6,000 men and women (about one third are women) here at the factory we're talking of are working rapidly. Walk about as I did and chat with them and you'll notice that even when they're joking with you their fine, quick hands never stop moving. When a voice calls through a loud-speaker, "It is twelve o'clock," they don't saunter toward the lunchroom. They run. At 12:25 they run back to their machines. They don't work sullenly. They work (I know it seems unbelievable) joyously, humming songs, joking with workers at the next bench, recounting the latest quip of Nat Gubbins or of Beachcomber, England's two favorite humorists. The head of the plant and I walked through the interminable lines of machines.

A foreman would shout above the clatter, "Hello, boss," and then go on working.

When the new fighter was ready for production the boss bet the five foremen of the five departments which were to build the aircraft one hundred dollars that the plane wouldn't be ready within three months. They finished it in sixty-three days and gleefully the boss handed out the five hundred dollars.

One foreman stopped work for a moment, "Thanks for that money, boss," he said smiling.

"I suppose you all got together and went on a pub crawl," the boss said.

"No," the foreman laughed, while the workers within earshot waited expectantly. They knew what was coming. "You see, boss, we got together and decided to give that money to Lord Beaverbrook's Spitfire Fund."

The boss rocked with laughter. "Pretty good aircraft, the Spitfire."

"We'll build better," the foreman said, and then bent over his machine. It was a machine for punching holes in steel and aluminum. On the side of it in bright red letters was the word "Cincinnati."

"That's a long way from home," I told the foreman.

"In the machine shop you'll find a few with 'Toledo' stamped on 'em," he grinned. "And we have a 'St. Louis' and a 'Detroit.' Good machines."

We walked on. Here was a room filled with aircraft which were practically completed. Even I recognized the Pratt and Whitney radial motors. "Good combination," the boss grinned. "English fuselage, American engines. It works just as well the other way around. Every aircraft that goes out of here has some American parts in it. Between us we can make pretty good airplanes."

This factory is one of the very few to use the production line or "track assembly" as it is called in England. The boss installed it a few years back and he says that it speeds up production twenty per cent. This is interesting in view of opinions expressed by American industrial leaders, and printed in English newspapers to the effect that the "belt system" would be impractical in the production of aircraft.

"I just studied a man named Ford," the boss said. "It worked well for him—why shouldn't it work well for me? Well, you can see for yourself."

The whole problem of mass production and of the assembly line can be summed up in one word—tools. This designer found out early that every time a new airplane was ready to start its long trip around the assembly line there was a cry from his works department for new tools. Now, as he bends over a drawing board working out a new design, he has one eye cocked toward the problem of the new jigs, cranes, wrenches, tools that will be needed. Even before his airplane is completed on the blueprints, machine shops are working feverishly to make the tools which will be needed. There is very little lost motion.

Such synchronization of effort and such co-operation can perhaps only come under the stress of a war emergency. At this factory the boss knows that everyone of his 6,000 workers has a tremendous pride in the product he is helping to create; he knows that his workers are loyal to England and to him. He can call on them for superhuman efforts, confident that they will arise to the need.

There is only one fundamental difference between ordinary group assembly and the track assembly method. In the first method the men move past the work; in the latter the work moves past the men. There is no lost motion. It certainly works in this factory. All this is elementary to anyone who has ever been in a Detroit automobile factory. In aircraft circles it is revolutionary.

The assembly line is really a track. Small carriages with heavy small wheels bear the weight of the aircraft. One line handles the fuselage; the other handles the undercarriage. They move slowly and men who know their jobs work deftly at their given tasks. The fuselage begins as an ugly skeleton. The undercarriage begins as a beetle on its back. The two wheels stick up like two legs. Gradually each takes shape. The fuselage begins to cover its nakedness after traveling thirty feet. It begins to look like an airplane.

The two lines finally meet and a huge crane lifts the fuselage into the air. The wheels and undercarriage slide forward. The fuselage is lowered. It is the work of twenty minutes to join them. Two men push the airplane forward thirty feet. Huge hangar doors are opened. The airplane, whole, complete, stands in the sun. Men come hurrying to attach long black hoses to the petrol tanks. Others put oil where oil should be put. Tommy or one of the other half-dozen test pilots hitches up his heavy parachute and climbs up on the wing and into the cockpit. He presses a button; he pulls back a throttle—and another airplane is ready to fight, or bomb, or train fledgling pilots. It is simple as that.

I have heard the heads of automobile companies wax lyrical about the synchronization and sheer beauty of well-managed mass production. It always left me cold. But then I'd never seen an automobile start as a tangle of white lines on a blueprint, I'd never watched it grow from a jumble of ugly parts into something compact and useful and beautiful. Now I can feel a little of what the automobile men feel. I've watched an airplane grow from a dream into a shining, poised, bright thing, and because so many of the machines used to create it and because so many of its parts now hidden by sleek wings and sides were of American make, perhaps the finished airplane meant more to me standing there on an English airdrome than it meant even to the designer or to the men who had built it. In any event, it's nice to see a dream (even a blueprint dream) come true.

I stayed in the factory until dark. The smells of the factory were interesting. The sharp, acid smell from the laboratory, the pungent odor of the milk-white fluid used to prevent drills from overheating, the various odors of the paints, and above all of these a pleasant scent of what seemed like banana oil.

The shift changed at five-thirty. Like a relief orchestra that replaces the main band so gradually that not a note is missed and not an interruption of the music noted. The new crew took over. The assembly line never stopped moving. It moves twenty-four hours a day; seven days a week. Beaverbrook sits dwarfed by a huge desk in the ministry of aircraft production. He knows that every two hours a new airplane emerges from the hangar doors of this factory. He knows that the same thing is happening all over England. Even he, the man who demands perfection, can find very little to complain about the aircraft production of the country.

I walked out into the night. A large aircraft landed and a dozen men hopped out. They were "ferry pilots." Their job was to take new planes to their particular destination. They wasted little time. They climbed into the new aircraft and without any fuss took off and flew away. It was a night of stars and high above a sickle moon gleamed. But it kept its light for its own grandeur, however; the heavy dark world beneath got very little of it. From the blacked-out factory there was the constant hum of machinery and occasionally the high screech of drills cutting through steel. Above there was the drone of the new airplanes winging their way toward battle; their motors singing a happy tribute to English industry.

CHAPTER NINETEEN

WEEK-END IN THE COUNTRY...

I MET NAT at the Savoy bar and he said, "How are things?"

"Things are great except that there's no light, no gas, and no water in my apartment," I told him.

"Come out to the country with me for a few days. We can play some golf," he suggested.

"I'd rather be bombed than bored," I said coldly, because that's how it is with golf and me. We just bore each other.

"You won't have to play golf," he said hastily, so I went with him. Nat and Mrs. Nat and their two children, Phil and Steve live at a place just thirty miles from London. The place has its equivalent thirty miles from New York, or Chicago or Detroit or Los Angeles. It is just another suburban com- muters' paradise. Ordinarily the men get the eight- ten train in the morning for London and come home on the five-five. Right now life isn't exactly normal in Nat's town. However, if war ever comes to Amer- ica places like Bronxville near New York and a thousand other suburban communities will find that life isn't quite normal either. A preview of life in Suburbia as it is in war time might prove interesting and a reflection of what life will be in suburban America should war come. So spend a couple of days with me visiting an ordinary English family living within commuting distance of London.

Nat hadn't been able to get through to his home on the telephone. Any telephone call in England is now an adventure. It is almost impossible to phone a town thirty miles outside of London unless you are transacting Government business.

In view of the fact that my hostess would have no warning I thought the shock of arrival might be broken if I brought her a present. In America I might have brought a bottle of wine, a box of candy, a dozen tennis balls. Instead I brought a twenty-pound roast beef. It is not easy to get beef in London. It is carefully rationed but I had been saving my coupons. When you do get it the cost is exactly thirty cents a pound—almost pre-war prices. There is no profiteering in food in London, though food prices have gone up about twelve per cent.

Nat and I hurried to Victoria Station to get the four-thirty train. We were told that the train was not running today. No one knew why. Apparently the track between London and his town had been bombed. There are several garages in London from which you can rent a car complete with driver. There is only one agency which will drive you after dark. The risk of injury to the car by bombs or shrapnel is too great. I managed to get a car and driver from this one garage.

We drove out through London. Sometimes we'd go a dozen blocks without seeing any sign of damage. Then we'd come to a place where a whole block of workers' flats had been leveled by a destruction bouquet dropped by the Nazi airmen. We passed churches and hospitals that gaped openly with only one or two walls standing.

"They are getting more accurate in their bombing," Nat said. "They've hit thirty hospitals in London so far."

"Two more this morning," I told him. "Anyone who goes to a hospital these days is crazy."

Finally the drab buildings of outer London were relieved by long stretches of country and then there would be a picturesque village. We were in Surrey, a county of long rolling hills which now were mottled with the bronzes and purples of autumn. We went through Nat's village. He lived just outside.

Mrs. Nat was glad to see us. So were the two girls Phil and Steve whose names were really Felicity and Stephania. Their ages were fifteen and thirteen.

"Your mother and two sisters are staying with us," Mrs. Nat said. He looked at her questioningly.

"A bomb hit their house this morning, darling," she said. "But none of them was hurt. In fact I think it's done Granny good. She wanted to stay and put out the fire."

We went into the house. Nat's mother was close to eighty. She was very, very annoyed at the German bombers but not at all frightened. Actually she was a bit superior to the bombs. The two children thought it a great lark—Granny's house being bombed.

"I'll phone and get you both rooms at the Country Club," Mrs. Nat. said. "You'll be quite comfortable."

It was cosy sitting in front of an open fire hearing Granny tell what she'd like to do to the Germans; hearing the excited and somewhat envious wonder of the children, a little jealous because until then their house had been the only one in the vicinity that had been hit.

"It was only an incendiary that hit us," Phil said with contempt. "It came right through the roof, though, and landed on Daddy's typewriter. It burned up all his books but that was all."

"Three other incendiaries landed in the garden," Nat said drily. "And my gentle wife went and put them out with a broom."

"Seems a nice quiet spot here in the country," I said.

"Now we'll have a cocktail," Nat's wife said with a fine sense of the practical. "We'll celebrate Granny getting bombed."

The problem of cocktails (important to any dweller in Suburbia) is not an easy one in England. There is a great shortage of vermouth so we don't have Martinis or Manhattans. There is a dearth, almost a famine, in lemons and there are no limes at all so we can't have rum cocktails. We compromised on gin and bottled lime juice.

My roast was brought out and duly admired and

it was decided to have it the following day. We'd
have chops tonight. Nat had a small garden, but
cauliflower, spinach, cabbage had replaced the tulips
and roses that had once blossemed there. That was
equally true of every home here in Suburbia. The
two girls served dinner. There was a cook but the
maid had left to drive an ambulance. Stevie brought
in a large platter on which there was a huge head
of cabbage.

"That looks like something Norman Hartnell
made for the Queen," I told Stevie.

"Don't talk about our Queen like that," Stevie
scolded. "She's wonderful."

I agreed that she was wonderful. So was the cabbage if you like cabbage. To me it's nothing but a
road company of cauliflower and you can have that
too.

After dinner we played games, the kind you'd play
in Bronxville or Scarsdale or at Lake Geneva. Then
the banshee wailed. The siren cut through the room
and no one talked until it had died out.

"Oh my," thirteen-year-old Phil sighed. "They're
up to their tricks again."

"Run along now," her mother said. This was a
nightly routine. The children stayed up until the
air warning sounded. Then they went to a shelter
Nat had built outside. I went to the shelter with
them. It was a fine shelter. The concrete was two
feet thick. It was built into a hill that rose steeply
in front of the garden. The girls were proud of their
shelter. There were four bunks in it and a sleeping

bag on the wooden floor. It had electric light and a radio and a row of books.

"Look at the funny books Daddy put in here," Stevie said.

The books were all appropriate to the occasion. There was *All This and Heaven Too, From Bad to Worse, Heaven's My Destination.*

"Are you coming for breakfast?" Stevie asked with a small anxious tone in her voice. I told her that I was.

"Do you want bacon and eggs for breakfast?" and now the anxiety had deepened. I told her that I didn't and she was much relieved.

"We could only get four eggs this week," she confided.

Eggs cost seven cents each when you can buy them. You seldom see an egg outside of a London hotel. Eggs and butter are scarcer than anything else. When a grocer in a village such as Nat's gets a consignment of eggs he distributes them equally to his regular customers. This week there were only four for Nat's family.

Two kittens frisked playfully about the shelter bouncing happily from bunk to bunk. One pounced frantically on a gas mask that lay on the bunk.

"I wish we could think of names for the kittens," Stevie said wistfully. "Their mother's name was Sally but we don't know what to call them."

"Call them Blitzie and Spitsie," I told them and the suggestion met with approval.

"I can tell a Spitfire from a Hurricane no matter

how high they are," Stevie said proudly. "A Spitfire
is low and straight and a Hurricane is a little bit
humpbacked. I used to be able to tell a Heinkel from
a Dornier but now Mother makes me come into the
shelter and I hardly ever see any fights. Have you
ever been in Hollywood?" she added irrelevantly.

When I told her that I had, she and her sister sat
down in anticipation of a long interrogation. "Whom
do you know in Hollywood?" they began.

"Bill Powell is a great friend of mine. So is Herbert Marshall and Jimmy Cagney and I was at the
front with Robert Montgomery driving in his ambulance. . . ." These magic names brought no light to
their eyes.

"Do you know Miss Shirley Temple?" Stevie asked
ominously.

"I have not the pleasure of Miss Shirley Temple's
acquaintance," I said with dignity, "but I know Joan
Bennett and Loretta Young and Ann Sheridan. . . ."
I was pulling names out of a hat desperately.

"Funny you never met Miss Shirley Temple," Phil
said a bit suspiciously.

"I guess she is too busy to see everyone who goes
to Hollywood," Stevie said, "but never mind."

"Next time I'm in Hollywood," I said weakly,
"I'll try to meet her." I felt I had lost considerable
caste. I went back into the house. Nat was now completely dressed in his Home Guard uniform. He
was wearing heavy boots and a huge heavy coat and
a forage hat and he had a heavy gun hung from his
side.

"I'll be out most of the night," he said. "We're having maneuvers tonight. A group of parachutists will land on Bridley Hill just before dawn. They usually land then, you know. They did in Holland and in Belgium. Our job is to capture them."

"Bring their parachutes home, dear, and I'll have them pressed," Nat's wife said. Then Nat kissed his family goodnight and we went to the Country Club. It was about half a mile away and we walked through the black night. The Germans were overhead en route to London. They go in waves so that it seems as if thousands are always up there. Nat's village was on the direct route to London. We looked towards London. High over the city brilliant golden stars were breaking against the black canopy of the night. But we knew these weren't stars. These were shells from the guns of London; helping to guard the people of London. We were thirty miles from the city. We couldn't hear the guns. But the stars kept appearing. London was having a tough night. Then suddenly the searchlights awoke from their sleep. Their white beams searched the skies. You had to pinch yourself to believe all this. We might be standing in Scarsdale now and watching these searchlights and bursting shells helping to guard New York. We knew that a lot of German planes were over London—the heightened activity of searchlights and shells told us that. We knew that bombs were raining down on London. For the moment I felt a bit disloyal as though I'd deserted the gallant

old city. But it was only for one night. I'd be back
again tomorrow.

Nat came in about five in the morning and he woke
me to say that they had captured the imaginary parachutists. But he was up at ten and we walked to his
home for breakfast. We had toast and coffee and
fruit. We could have had bacon. A neighbor had
wanted some tea so she and Nat's wife did a bit of
bartering. Nat's wife got a pound of bacon in exchange for six ounces of tea. Barter is common now
in English villages. The two children had been out
for some time, Mrs. Nat explained, collecting money
for the local Spitfire Fund.

"They haven't been to school for eight months,"
she said. "The hard thing is to keep them busy.
There are of course a few schools open, but they have
hit so many schools lately I'd rather keep them home
with me."

If you are a mother in a London suburban town
you must be teacher, cook, fire fighter, nurse, all at
once. Mothers in America may one day be faced with
the same problem and will undoubtedly rise to the
occasion as have the mothers of England. The two
girls returned happy because they had collected one
pound ten (six dollars).

"There are some new people down the road in
the big red house," Stevie explained excitedly, "And
the woman said she wouldn't give anything to the
Spitfire Fund because she was a pacifist. I said 'Well,
you aren't very patriotic then,' and she said, 'I cer-

tainly am. I would gladly play hockey for England.'
And do you know what Phil said to her? Phil said,
'Well, if it weren't for the Spitfires you'd probably
be playing hockey for Germany right now.' "

"Phil, Phil," her mother reproached, but Nat and
I thought it was funny and even Mrs. Nat had to
laugh. Laughter is a great weapon these days in England and children are lucky enough to have it in
abundance.

"Could I have your cigarette package when you're
through with it?" Stevie asked.

I only had two cigarettes left. I took them out of
the package and gave the package to Stevie. She
was very happy about it.

"I have saved about four pounds of tinfoil so far,"
she said separating the tinfoil from the paper. "Phil
saves paper and tin. I save tinfoil and iron. Our village has sent Lord Beaverbrook enough tinfoil and
iron and paper to build two Spitfires."

I didn't like to ask what part of a Spitfire was
made of paper. The kids left, busy with plans to
collect more iron, paper, tin. All over England
youngsters are doing the same. England has elimi-
nated waste. When we typewrite stories or letters we
use both sides of the paper. Scraps of food are saved
and if not usable in the kitchen are given to a farmer
who owns pigs. We don't throw used matches away.
The wood can be used again. It is not fashionable
to be wasteful in England.

The front bell rang. Three Canadian soldiers stood
there smiling. There was a large contingent of Cana-

dians nearby. Every home in the village had been
thrown open to them so that they could have hot
baths every day. They'd just finished a long hike and
they were muddy.

Nat's wife said, cheerfully, "Go right upstairs,
boys. There's lots of hot water. And there'll be tea
ready when you come down."

"Aren't they a nuisance?" I asked Nat's wife.

"Nuisance? I should say not," she exploded. "They
are grand lads. I sometimes have as many as twenty
a day in for baths and they're the finest boys you ever
saw. God knows there's little enough we can do for
them. The least we can do is to give them hot water."

After their baths they came down and had their
tea. We sat and talked of Montreal and of Toronto
and always they talked of going back "after we've
licked the Jerries." As they were leaving one of them
said to Nat, "Your wife has been mighty kind to
us. Wish there was something we could do in return.
Have you a place where you could hang a heifer?"

Nat was startled, "Good heavens, no. And where
would you ever get a heifer?"

The soldier was a bit embarrassed. "Well, a few
miles from here there's a farmer who has more damn
cows. He'd never miss just one."

Nat assured him that the household, couldn't use
a heifer. They left and Nat and I got out his car and
drove to the village. Ordinarily we would have
walked but Nat had hiked fifteen miles during the
night and his feet hurt. A lifetime of sitting in front
of a typewriter hadn't exactly fitted him for long

hikes. We walk a great deal in England. Nat was allowed about five gallons of gasoline a week—that was all. So the car was saved for emergency duty.

We parked in front of the local pub and Nat raised the hood of the car and took out the distributor. He slipped in into his pocket. Everyone does that in England. You can get a summons for parking your car without removing the distributor. When parachutists landed in Holland, Belgium and northern France, they immediately grabbed all automobiles within sight. They had mechanics with them so it didn't matter if the cars were locked. But once the distributor is removed it takes more than a mechanic to start a car. If Herr Hitler finally decides to land parachutists in this country he will find that the army of the people, the civilians, will be ready for them.

We went into the pub, which was warm and cosy. It was three hundred years old. The dignified old gentleman who stood behind the bar looked almost that old too. His name was Mr. Adams and everyone called him Mr. Adams.

"I just heard about your mother's house being hit yesterday," he said quietly. "Now the missus and I have a large spare room upstairs with plenty of blankets and a nice fire. We'd be happy, sir, to have your mother and sisters move in with us. I know your own house is pretty crowded."

Nat said, "That's good of you. But it's all right."

Mr. Adams poured us our beer and he added earnestly, "Any time, don't fail to call on me."

Two middle-aged men, obviously farm laborers, came in and one tipped his hat to Nat. "It being Saturday, me and my mate are off this afternoon. I heard they made a bit of a mess at your mother's house. We'd be glad to go up and straighten things out."

"It's all right," Nat said gently. "The lads have already fixed everything up."

We all drank beer in companionable silence and I was thinking of people I knew in suburban towns around New York and I was wondering if they would react in these circumstances as these men and women were reacting.

We walked out of the pub and stood there in the crisp autumn air. Up the road was the village school; across from it the village church and here the pub. These three things are symbols of what England is fighting to maintain. The pub in many ways is more important than the other two; it is the place where men gather to speak their minds. The pub is the symbol of free speech in England.

"You English are pretty swell people, Nat," I said. "I guess you're our kind of people all right."

"Yes," Nat said thoughtfully and then like any Englishman afraid of sentiment he growled, "You might have known Miss Shirley Temple, though. You let the kids down badly."

CHAPTER TWENTY

NOBODY'S BETTER OFF DEAD . . .

THE AMBULANCE STOPPED and there was an air
warden standing there. He pointed silently. The two
girls hopped down from the ambulance and ran into
the air shelter. I followed them. This had been a
tannery once but it was now an air shelter in the
East End of London.

We went in, closed the doors and lit our searchlights. People came, ghostlike, out of the shadow
and surrounded us. The two girl ambulance drivers
were very businesslike. This was routine to them.

"Where is he?" one of them said.

Two of them led a huge, fair-haired man toward
us. He was muttering angrily. There was a bandage
on his head and one on his wrist. When one of the
girls grabbed his wounded arm he pulled it away.

"He got hit by shrapnel on the head and on his
wrist," one of the men explained. "Then he stumbled
in here. But there's something funny about him. He's
got no papers. Where are your papers?"

"Lost," the tall man said dully.

More figures appeared from the shadows. There were low mutterings. He had no papers. He spoke with a funny accent. Who was he? The girls tried to lead him out into the street and into the ambulance. He wouldn't go. Said he was afraid of the bombs and of the shrapnel. He wanted to stay where he was. He shouted it because bombs were falling near the docks which were close by and the anti-aircraft batteries were sending up a lot of heavy stuff. It was very noisy.

"Make him go along," someone said. "Why ain't he any papers?" "Who is he?" They were angry at the man. You carry your identification papers in London just as you wear your shoes. "Before you came he was yelling something in some foreign language. Sounded like German," someone said.

Our small flashlights cut the darkness and grotesque shadows chased after one another on the walls. These people didn't understand the man, therefore they were afraid of him, and being afraid of him they were angry at him. Fear hung limply in the heavy air of the place that had been a tannery.

The tall man was muttering again and I bent close to hear what he was saying. He was talking German, which was no language to talk in the middle of the East End during a particularly terrible air raid. But when he spoke I knew two things about him: first, he was a Belgian and second, he was drunk.

"You're a policeman," one of the men from the shadows said to me. "Why don't you hit him one?"

"I'm not a policeman," I told him.

"Well, you look like a policeman," he growled.

I told the two girl ambulance drivers that the man was a Belgian sailor and that he was drunk. Then I took the bandage off the man's head and the girls saw that it wasn't much of a wound at all. Neither was the shrapnel wound on his wrist. The girls told him sharply to go to the nearest police station. They'd dress his silly wounds there. The girls told the people in the shelter who he was, and now the fear that had hung heavily in the air disappeared and everything was all right. He'd just got drunk and lost his papers.

"And us thinking him a blasted Jerry," someone laughed.

We went outside and the moon was very full and there were no clouds. We climbed into the ambulance and drove back to the station. This was all routine to these girl ambulance drivers.

They were part of the London Auxiliary Ambulance Service. They were two of 150,000 women who are on duty each night in London.

Their station was in a garage. Back of the garage was the dugout where they stayed between calls. They called it a dugout but actually it was an artificial shelter made out of sandbags. The sandbags on all four sides were four feet thick. Three feet of sandbags covered the roof. The dugout was thirty feet long and eight feet wide. Inside it looked like a sandbagged trench. There was a table and on it a telephone and an electric stove on which a kettle was boiling. The woman in charge of this station sat behind the table. Sixteen other women sat on long

benches that ran the length of the dugout. The two
girls made their report to the woman in charge.

They all laughed about the drunken Belgian sailor
who had lost his papers. They laughed about me
being mistaken for a policeman.

They all wore the blue uniform of the L.A.A.S.
Half of these girls were drivers, the other half at-
tendants. When the phone rang it meant that there
was trouble. When it rang the two girls who were
up next stood and walked to the table. Then quietly,
casually, they walked out to the garage, climbed into
an ambulance and set out through deserted but noisy
streets on their errand. Six nights a week, four weeks
a month, these girls do this job.

Things were active in the East End this night.
They usually are. Occasionally we heard the planes
over us and then we'd hear the angry symphony of
the air barrage rising to a crescendo.

"There's George," one of the girls shouted cheerfully. A German plane is "Jerry" to everyone in
London. These girls call it George and they didn't
know why either. Now through the sharp roar of
the air barrage we heard the sound of the bombs.
They were fairly close and then there was a terrific
explosion and the dust from the sandbags filled the
dugout and got into our eyes.

No one said anything. The noise and the concussion from a bomb that falls close stun you for a
moment.

"That was quite near," the woman in charge said
calmly.

"Let's see if it hit the school," one of the girls said. It was a high-explosive bomb and it had landed in the schoolyard next to the garage. It landed exactly one hundred paces from our dugout. There was a large crater in the schoolyard but no fire. We went back to our dugout.

We all had fresh tea because the dust from the sandbags had gotten into our teacups and dust is no good in tea. The girls relaxed, some sitting on the wooden benches, some sitting on the floor. There was an alarm clock on the table. The alarm clock said 11:30. Someone said: "The clock has stopped. Actually it's just midnight."

The woman in charge laughed. "The concussion from the bomb stopped it." She shook it, reset it, wound it and it began to tick on merrily.

"An American alarm clock," I said complacently. "Even a bomb can't hurt it."

"An English clock wouldn't even have stopped," one of the girls hooted.

A slightly built girl walked into the dugout. She took off her blue service hat and said to the woman in charge, "I'd like to work tonight."

"But, Ethel, dear," the woman said, "this is your night off. Why aren't you home in bed?" Then she looked at Ethel and stopped. And for some reason everyone stopped talking.

"When I got home this morning," the girl said, "I found I didn't have any home. I want to work tonight. Let me be first out, please."

The woman in charge was marvelous and understanding. The rest of us sat in silence. The woman in charge said casually, "Yes, Ethel, you and Pringle go out next."

Ethel sat down on the wooden bench. No one asked her any questions.

In the silence the kettle began to hum. Tea is more than a drink in London; it's a symbol of sanity and a reminder of days that were normal and that days will be normal again. One of the girls handed Ethel a cup of tea. "By the way, Ethel," the woman in charge said quietly, "Wyndham Street was hit earlier this evening. It is full of glass. If you get a call in that section keep to the side streets."

Soon the girls started to talk again. They talked of small things, as girls do. A few of them still keep their jobs during the daytime. They grab what sleep they can here in the dugout. The phone rang and everybody was quiet. Ethel and the girl they called Pringle got up. The woman in charge gave crisp directions. They set off.

Then it rang again. "Yes, I've got it. Yes, East End Avenue. Right away." She put down the phone. "Harris and Foster are up. Fire on East End Avenue."

They left and the woman in charge said, "I think I'll take a car and go along. That's a residential neighborhood. May need more than one ambulance. Care to come?"

I nodded. The woman in charge, who made me promise I wouldn't use her name, could drive. But then it was light. It was the kind of night poets sing about. We curse bright nights when the moon is full. On a night like this the Thames would be a white ribbon of milk pointing toward London. You can't black-out the Thames and the Thames tells the German bombers everything they want to know about London.

The streets were deserted of course. This seemed like a dead city except for the noise. The anti-aircraft guns were hurling up thousands of tons of defensive armor and the shell broke high against the stars in sharp, golden flashes. Bombs were falling and the combined noise of the guns and bombs seemed to tear the energy and life from you and make you feel very tired. We sped along and now even above the guns we heard the shattering of glass.

"I told Ethel to avoid this street," the woman in charge said. "And now I go right into it myself."

We drove over glass for three blocks. It was a street of small shops. All had been shattered. Air-raid wardens, home guards and the police were all too busy for the moment to start clearing the street of glass. We crunched over the glass and miraculously didn't get a blowout. Then we hurried on past it. We came to East End Avenue. We turned right and saw the fire. A high wind had come up and the sparks were flying all over the night. The firemen were playing two streams of water on the house.

We saw the white ambulance in front of the burning house. It was a nice one, in a row of good, substantial three-story brick houses. We walked up close to the house. I had borrowed one of the tin hats from the dugout. The ambulance girls wear steel helmets with a large black "A" emblazoned on them. No one asks questions when you wear one of these. We just walk in. We walked into the courtyard in front of the house.

The bomb had hit directly and apparently had fallen through the house into the cellar, where it exploded. The firemen concentrated on the bottom of the house. There were perhaps a dozen firemen, four policemen, a couple of air-raid wardens and ourselves there. The rest of the street was deserted. People don't "go to fires" in London. The upper two floors were burning fiercely. But the water had nearly killed the fire in the cellar. Two firemen, shielding their faces from the heat, walked into the building. I crouched down and looked through a broken window into the cellar. The firemen were down there.

"All dead," one of them shouted.

"Maybe not," the other said. Then he called: "Stretchers."

The girls had the stretchers ready. They handed them through the broken window to the firemen in the cellar. Soon the two firemen came out of the building carrying a stretcher. They laid it down. There was a doctor there now. The woman didn't look dead. The doctor had a needle ready and he stuck it into the flesh just below her heart. Then he bent over and began to give her the kind of artificial respiration that lifeguards give.

The firemen came out with another stretcher. The doctor hesitated for a moment and the woman in charge of our ambulance group said, "All right, I'll carry on."

This was a woman too. She looked about thirty. The doctor gave her an injection. The doctor had a stethoscope around his neck. It was a white stethoscope so that he could find it easily in the dark. As he worked the arms of the woman rhythmically back and forth the white stethoscope swung to and fro from his chest.

"Take this damn' thing. It keeps falling over my eyes," the woman in charge said to me and she handed me her steel helmet. She kept on giving the woman artificial respiration. The firemen brought another stretcher out. This, too, was a woman. She was dead. I never want to see that again—someone who has been burned to death.

I stood up and went to the doorway of the house. A fireman came out. "Didn't need the stretcher for this one," he said. He had a child in his arms. The child had long golden hair and, strangely, it hadn't been touched. The fireman walked out of the courtyard and laid the child on the street. The doctor came hurrying over. The child was about three. She couldn't be dead. She was asleep. I turned away when the doctor pressed the needle. I suppose there was adrenalin in the needle.

The fire was crowning the top of the house. It would be out soon but it was flaring up obscenely as though glorying in the thing it had done this night. I walked a little away from the house. A man and his wife were standing there. They lived next to the burning building and the firemen had gotten them out.

I asked them about the three women and the child. They told me their names. The youngest was married and it was her child the doctor was working on. The other two women were her sisters. I asked why there weren't any men in the house.

"Her husband is in the army," the man said briefly.

"There's Jerry again," one of the firemen said.

We knew he'd come again at night. He could see this burning house at 20,000 feet. We heard the uneven hum of his motors and then the roar of the air barrage keeping him high, keeping him dodging shrapnel so that he couldn't get a good shot at us. The searchlights suddenly snapped on.

"Why does he bomb here?" I asked one of the policemen. "No targets around here, are there?"

He pointed down the street. "See that building?" he said. "That's what he's after."

It was so bright that I could plainly see the huge building. "What is it?" I asked.

"It's a hospital. One of the largest in London," the policeman said. "He's been after it for three nights."

Jerry was dropping his bombs but he was missing us. One of the firemen was working over the child now. The doctor was in the courtyard.

"Put these three women into the ambulance," he said.

One of the girls said, "Shall I take them to the hospital, doctor?"

He shook his head. "No," he said wearily.

There was only the child left. The doctor bent over her again. There wasn't a burn on her tiny body. The doctor put his arms underneath her and lifted her up a foot.

"Keep her head down," he said.

I held the head down and the golden curls were soft to touch. I found myself saying, "Wake up, wake up, wake up."

She couldn't be dead. She was asleep. I've seen three-year-old girl children asleep and this is how they sleep. A three-year-old child always sleeps with a faint frown on her face as though daring anyone to wake her. This child was sleeping like that.

The doctor reached for her arms again. I stood up. The ambulance with the three bodies in it rumbled away—not to the hospital.

I know this isn't a pleasant chapter to read. It isn't a pleasant one to write. It's much better to read and write about the fighting pilots, the "gay, laughing-eyed knights of the air." Sure, that's what war is. Glamorous and exciting. If death comes, well, it is swift and clean. War? Why, war is a line of gallant British battleships plowing through azure waters with flags flying and bands playing and a tot of rum for the lads on watch at night. Sure, that's what war is.

But that isn't the war I see in London every night. This is the war I see. If you want a front seat to the war come and stand over this three-year-old child with me. Don't be afraid of the bombs that are falling close or the spent shrapnel that is raining down on us. You want to see what war is really like, don't you? Take another look at the baby. She still looks as though she were asleep. This is war—fall style, 1940. This is the war that Herr Hitler is waging.

Finally the doctor stood up. The fire had burned itself out now. A murky grayness was lighting the sky. Dawn had come to banish the horror of the night. The German bombers are creatures of the night. They fade before the light of the dawn and scurry back to their own airdromes. The doctor shook his head wordlessly and then the scream of the siren cut through the dawn. It was the steady sound telling us that the German bombers had gone.

"All clear," the doctor muttered ironically. "Well, they've done their work. Why shouldn't they go home?"

He bent and lifted the child in his arms. He walked to the ambulance with her. He placed her on a stretcher and put a blanket over her. He didn't cover her face. It still wore that little frown.

"Maybe she's better off dead," he said.

I shook my head. "Nobody's better off dead," I told him.

CHAPTER TWENTY-ONE

IT'S NOISY TONIGHT...

WORDS ARE LIKE CORDIALS—too many of them make you sick. Reading too many words, writing too many words, hearing too many words—it's all the same. Now I've written too many words and I'm sick of words.

But in London there is an antidote. You can be jerked back from the unreality of what you are writing by merely stopping your typewriter. All writing is unreal because what you've written has already happened and therefore is dead and only the living are real. I've always felt that once you've read a book that book is dead. I hate to have my room cluttered up with dead books.

No book ever written can equal the drama that is going on tonight in London. A city of six million people is crouching underground; not cowering with fear, but crouching for safety. Babies are being born in shelters under the earth. Men and women are dying as I write this. It is what we call a very "noisy" night in London. Perhaps a hundred German planes are over London now looking for places (if they do look for places) to drop their bombs. If they don't find what they are looking for they'll drop them anywhere. Two landed here in Berkeley Square, less than an hour ago. The first one killed two air raid wardens. There are a dozen fires burning in London now; I put out my lights and drew back my black curtains to see.

Gradually they are chipping away at London as a woodman chips away at a tree. They are trying to kill London. You can kill a tree by chopping it down. You can kill a book by reading it. You can't kill London by destroying the buildings of London. The bombs that are falling tonight are destroying buildings and killing people. But a bomb has its limitations. A bomb can only destroy buildings and kill people.

A bomb cannot kill the spirit of a people who have been through the greatest mass torture any people have ever been asked to endure. Tonight, except for the fires, London is dark and you could walk for five miles through the streets of London without meeting anyone. You might think that London was a ghost city tonight if you didn't know better. You might say that the city slept or even that it was dead.

But those of us who have lived through the past months with the people of London know better. London is more alive tonight than it has ever been in its history. In the morning London will count its dead and then face the new day. London is fighting for its existence. London can never die as long as the spirit of London lives. No bomb, no land mine has yet been devised which is capable of killing this spirit.

And so, knowing this, we laugh a little at the bombs. They try so hard and accomplish so little. They crush our homes; they stun us with their concussion; they kill our neighbors but that's all that they can do. The buildings can be rebuilt; the concussion gives us nothing but headaches; our neighbors are all prepared to die.

But no one in London town is prepared to surrender. Even those who have been cut and mangled by the screaming tons of iron which have fallen on London tonight endure their agony. These civilians of London are good soldiers. London has been hurt tonight and will be hurt again tomorrow night, and every night thereafter. But no one is crying. Not even the wounded. The wounded don't cry.

THE END.